Archery for All

More and more people are taking up archery every year; clubs
are flourishing; archery itself is an Olympic sport. Daniel Roberts,
a club instructor, gives sound basic advice to the beginner in
a delightfully informal and humorous style. He points out that
archery is not expensive, nor does it require exceptional athletic
skill. It can be enjoyed the year round, both in and out of doors.
This is an invaluable guide to what the author calls the 'tranquil
strength' of shooting straight with bow and arrow—an art which
can never grow stale or boring.

Widen Your Horizons with this new series

Remember that we cater for all interests. See for yourself with our expanding list of titles.

Places to see

Scottish Islands — Tom Weir
Dartmoor — Crispin Gill

Leisure Activities

Railways for Pleasure — Geoffrey Body
Good Photography Made Easy — Derek Watkins
Looking at Churches — David Bowen

Sporting

The Art of Good Shooting — J. E. M. Ruffer

Holidays

Canoe Touring — Noel McNaught

Forthcoming titles

Exmoor — Colin Jones
Sea Fishing for Fun — Alan Wrangles
A Guide to Safe Rock Climbing — Patrick Scrivenor
Rowing for Everyone — Christopher Chant

Archery for All

Daniel Roberts

Illustrations by
Doreen Roberts

David & Charles
Newton Abbot   London
North Pomfret (VT)   Vancouver

ISBN 0 7153 7189 4

Set in 11 on 13 Bembo
and printed in Great Britain
by Redwood Burn Limited, Trowbridge & Esher
for David & Charles (Publishers) Limited
Brunel House   Newton Abbot   Devon

Published in the United States of America
by David & Charles Inc
North Pomfret   Vermont 05053   USA

Published in Canada
by Douglas David & Charles Limited
1875 Welch Street   North Vancouver   BC

Contents

1   **A Tranquil Strength**   6

2   **Variety**   8
Target archery – field archery – flight shooting – archery
golf – clout shooting – popinjay – huntin' an' fishin' –
novelty shoot – a programme for the year

3   **Equipment**   17
Buying equipment in three stages

4   **Shooting**   46
Where and when – how – standard technique – what
champions are made of – personal first-aid in technique –
other techniques

5   **The Club**   70
Joining a club – forming a new club – established clubs –
archery in schools

6   **Target Business**   95
The Rounds – scoring – classification scheme and handicap system – tournaments – governing bodies of archery
– some records

7   **A Short History of Archery**   110
The weapon – the sport

Glossary   118

Appendix   121

Further Reading   122

Acknowledgements   123

Index   125

1 A Tranquil Strength

Every year, more and more people take to pony trekking, and every year, more and more people take to canoeing, sailing, surfing, rock-climbing, pot-holing, ski-ing and other sports where the influence of natural surroundings combined with a test of our abilities bring back a kind of tranquil strength we had forgotten could exist. Archery, too, satisfies our longings for active enjoyment and sanity; and archery has its own brand of magic. Once under its spell, you will never again be free.

What makes archery so captivating and so approachable? Is it easy? The answer is a definite NO. People who have never handled a bow drop the 'Ha, ha, Robin Hood stuff' attitude after shooting only a few arrows. Crack rifle shots are often surprised at the ease with which they repeatedly miss the target at a mere twenty yards, while athletic six-footers sometimes seem unable to draw a beginner's bow! But the attractions of archery are many. One in particular is difficult to describe without making the reader smile or even laugh outright. One would have to use words like 'spiritual', 'psychic', 'race memory', etc, but only a gifted poet should attempt to express the deep, somewhat strange thrill that comes from shooting in a good bow.

More simply, there is the satisfaction of being in control of a deadly weapon while using it for peaceful enjoyment; there is the rewarding struggle with oneself to achieve muscle and mental discipline, the constant challenge of improving one's scores at various distances, the peace of green lawns, the benefit to one's health, and – but a long list becomes tedious, even if it be made up of the best things in the world. Perhaps one could vary the eulogy with a few negatives.

Archery need not be expensive, nor does it require exceptional athletic ability. As long as you have two good arms, one good eye and can breathe, you can be an archer. There is no restriction in age, and young ladies need not worry about developing unsightly biceps; the only change in their physique will be an even more graceful bearing. Archery is not necessarily a holiday sport; it can be practised the whole year round, indoors as well as out of doors. There are over 670 clubs in England, and the 10,000-odd British toxophilities are always glad to welcome and help newcomers.

This book is not a manual for advanced archers, nor a scholarly treatise. Its main ambition is to help new clubs and to give some up-to-date information about archery in Britain. It is also aimed at the countless number of 'might-be' archers; if it can change the 'might-be' into 'will-be', it will have succeeded.

2 Variety

Two misconceptions often arise from a lack of first-hand experience: one, that archery is a child's game and that grown-ups 'playing' with bows and arrows must be slightly dotty, to say the least; and two, that archery must very soon become tedious. 'Don't you get bored, shooting at the same target day after day?'

Bored! Target archery cannot be boring because every practice and every match is a new challenge, with a ceaseless striving towards improvement; and besides conventional archery there are at least seven other types of archery with which to refresh oneself after too long a spell of 'target bashing'. According to your temperament, time of year or location, you can choose between:

Target Archery

This is the most common form of archery in Europe. The target used is a circular straw boss 4ft in diameter, covered with a brightly coloured face which is divided into five or ten concentric 'zones' with the centre, or 'pinhole', standing 4ft 3in above the ground (see fig 1).

A beginnner will stand at about 20yd from the target and shoot at longer distances as his skill improves. As soon as he reaches a reasonable standard he will take part in club 'rounds' (see Chapter 6).

British Rounds are shot on five-zone faces. The centre is called the 'Gold' (never 'bull's eye'), then comes red, blue, black, white and – about half an inch of 'petticoat' which has no scoring value at all. Beyond that it would appear that you have missed the target, but this expression being too coarse for such a gentlemanly sport, one speaks of an arrow being 'dropped' or having 'hit the green'.

While the unseasoned archer will shoot the short Rounds, usually 6 or 9 dozen arrows, the experienced shots will practise the long Rounds (12 dozen arrows) at distances of 100, 80 and 60yd. An archer shooting the 144 arrows of a York Round, using a 42lb bow would, by the end of the day, have drawn the equivalent of 12,600lb. Did somebody say 'child's game'?

Shooting the Rounds allows you to assess your progress and to take part in competitions like club matches or county tournaments. Thanks to a handicap system, you will be able to compete against experienced archers. When your scores improve, you will eventually reach the status of 3rd, 2nd or 1st class Archer and even, perhaps, that of Master Bowman or Grand Master Bowman!

The climax to target archery is, of course, the first tournament – a line of 30 to 40 targets; 100 or more archers dressed in white and green; a peaceful, often beautiful setting; all this, given good weather, makes for an unforgettable day.

Field Archery

Field shooting is widely practised in the USA and in Sweden, and is growing fast in Britain. The British Field Association has been given grants to develop its field course in the Rhondda Valley for national

Peaceful, often beautiful settings – Arundel Castle grounds

and international events. This type of archery was first devised to keep your eye in for hunting; it is back-to-nature in a big way, shooting through woods and dales, across streams and lakes and up and down hills. The style or technique is different from that of Target shooting; stronger bows and longer arrows with longer fletching are used.

Field archers move from target to target, a 'unit' being made up of fourteen targets, varying in size, and at different distances. For the 'Hunters Round', for instance, you are supposed to hit two 6in faces at distances of 5 to 15yd, four 12in faces from 10 to 30yd, five 18in faces from 20 to 40yd and three 24in faces from 30 to 50yd.

While it would be a pretty poor club which could not find a location for target archery, the same cannot be said for real field archery. At least 7 acres are needed, 14 being preferable. You will also need to be fit and strong, not mind shooting in rough or cold weather and be prepared to work on the upkeep of the course. Keen 'target' archers do not often seem attracted by field archery, while converts to field archery will come out of their woods in the summer to have a go at the big target. To shoot well in both demands a degree of adaptability which is, undoubtedly, a mark of the true archer.

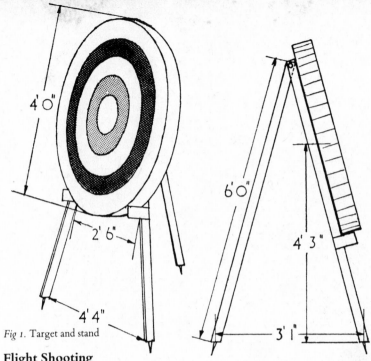

Fig 1. Target and stand

Flight Shooting

This is purely concerned with distance: you shoot your arrow to see how far it can go. A certain eighteenth-century Turkish Sultan shot an arrow 972yd. It took 200 years to beat this record, now held by the American free-style archer Harry Drake, whose arrow remained airborne for 1,100yd!

Competitions in flight shooting are divided into three classes; target bows, flight bows (much shorter and more powerful) and free style. In the last, you may lie on your back if you wish, rest your bow on your feet and draw with both hands. You may thus establish a record, but you will also deal a severe blow to the grace and dignity of archery. Still, there is great enjoyment to be had in flight shooting; indeed, it is our first instinct, as a boy with our first home-made bow, to see how far we can shoot rather than aim at anything in particular. Adults who pursue this kind of archery will do so mainly from technical interest, experimenting with new equipment, always striving to improve its power.

Archery Golf

This is again more popular in the United States than in Britain.

Perhaps, if more golf club secretaries could be encouraged to take up archery, the sport would spread. As a break from target archery, it is ideal, for it combines the excitement of competition with the pleasures of instinctive shooting on varied grounds. With the wide open gentle views of a golf course and shots up to 250yd, it has a distinct character of its own. For maximum enjoyment, it should be played on a proper golf course, with teams of archers against golfers. The cast from a good target bow and a long golf drive being roughly the same, the players fight on equal terms except, perhaps, in high winds, when the archers have a definite advantage.

When the players reach the putting green, the archers will 'hole out' by hitting a 4in cardboard disc on the ground, pop a small balloon or shoot through a ring. For the low angle shots on the green, a special spike is added to the arrow to avoid its skidding on the turf and vanishing in the rough.

But, in spite of the somewhat natural reserve from golf club secretaries, golfers and archers have, in fact, been challenging each other for some time. The first match on record was played in 1842. More recently (1969), twelve archers challenged fourteen golfers to a duel that lasted 4 hours and covered about 8 miles over the Ashdown Forest. The archers won.

Clout Shooting

I wonder how many tired club instructors have dreamt of inventing a new version of 'shooting the clout', with a simple alteration in the spelling! Actually, 'clout' was the old English word for 'cloth'. A white cloth was laid on the ground and archers had to hit it from distances of 160, 200 or 240yd.

Clout shooting is still practised today, but the white cloth has been replaced by a flag, and scoring within five landing zones is kept with the help of a marked rope pivoted round the flag post, or with white rings. Men shoot at 9 score yards and ladies at 6 score yards. It makes an amusing change and is also good practice for golf archery.

Popinjay

This game reached England from the Continent via Scotland some six centuries ago, and is still popular in Belgium. It consists of shooting up at wooden birds fixed on top of a high pole. A special blunt head is added to the arrow for at least two obvious reasons: it would be uneconomical to damage the popinjay, and the arrows will come down again.

On the 85ft mast stands the cock bird with resplendent plumage and a 10 to 12in body, then a row of hen birds 6 or 8in tall and one or possibly two rows of chicks 3 or 4in tall. The GNAS (Grand National Archery Society) 'roost' is made up of one cock, four hens and three rows of chicks numbering respectively seven, eight and nine birds. The archers draw for the order of shooting and shoot one arrow in turn. They, and the spectators must keep their eye on the return flight if they want to avoid meeting the splashdown head on.

Although popinjay shooting is exciting fun, it has one great drawback: the cost of the mast and birds.

Huntin' An' Fishin'

Sixteenth-century ladies shot at deer kept in enclosures so that *'they might readily shoot at them without the trouble and fatigue of rousing and pursuing them'*. Most modern women will agree that the suffering inflicted on straw targets is not quite so disturbing, and a well anchored boss does not usually need 'rousing and pursuing'. If, however, you have the urge to destroy beautiful wild creatures, you will find hunting with a bow a rewarding sport. Stalking the quarry demands the ancient skills of silence, patience and endurance, and the archer must be a good shot or hours of walking and waiting will be wasted. But archery hunting in Britain is hardly worth the candle. It is still illegal to shoot a deer with an arrow, although you will no longer have your hand amputated if you are caught. It leaves one, therefore, with the odd rabbit or sleepy pheasant; and by the time you have missed and lost two or three arrows, you will begin to think it would have been cheaper to go to the butcher's. (If you are shooting at small game in trees, a blunt head on the arrows and 'flu' fletching will ensure that your arrows come down again in a vertical drop.)

Hunting in the US or in Africa is a different story altogether. There, with bows of up to 100lb draw and arrowheads as sharp as razors, you can, in many areas, kill virtually anything. A famous American hunter shot an elk dead at 180yd and, among other animals, killed four elephants (penetration: 14in, death instantaneous by haemorrhage). Films show bow hunters felling charging lions with one arrow between the eyes, but one wonders how many guns stood at the ready behind the cameraman and bowman. In the United States, boar, goat and deer, let alone birds and smaller animals, are targets for bowhunters.

For fishing, a reel has to be fixed on to the bow and a barbed head to the arrow. Although the range is seldom more than 20 or 25ft, it requires a good deal of experience to compensate for light refraction.

Novelty Shoots

This heading is apt to raise a supercilious smile on the purist's face, and he will murmur 'Stunts!' Yet the Japanese archers who shoot at small targets while galloping on horseback or speeding on skis must be undeniably skilful. It will be some time, though, before British archers can combine these sports with such a high degree of expertise.

Novelty shoots are, on the whole, meant to amuse the spectators at archery displays. Popping balloons is a favourite and, with a good wind, it can test the best archers. Shooting an apple off a dummy's head, noughts and crosses, darts (dartchery) and even archery cricket, all are light entertainment and bring a welcome change to the sustained concentration of target archery. Matches against rifle and pistol clubs can be arranged, and out-door midnight shoots in artificial light and a somewhat eerie atmosphere have been held. Some clubs are known to organise a yearly 'Medieval' or 'Victorian' meeting with everyone dressed in period.

With a little imagination, all kinds of novelty shoots can be improvised, like, for instance, finishing off an old target by shooting flaming arrows at it. This was actually done by a factory archery club. But when they succeeded at last in setting the thing ablaze, a fire engine appeared on the scene and put it out forthwith!

A Programme for the Year

It seems clear, from this simple glance at the manifold aspects of archery, that a club could shoot practically the whole year round without any reason or excuse for staleness.

Ruling out the possibility that clubs should spring up in areas totally devoid of flat land, we shall assume that most societies will want to start with *Target Archery*, its obvious advantage being the large number of events in which archers of all ages and standards can

Disbelieving knight – medieval shoot

participate. It is also easier to begin with a form of archery where you stand well poised on level ground, aiming at a nice big target directly before you. However, except for a few doggedly striving towards the coveted badges of Master or Grand Master Bowman or for a County Flash, most target archers will benefit from an occasional change in routine.

From late spring to mid-autumn, monthly or bi-monthly shoots of the 'novelty' kind could replace the usual Club Rounds. Different kinds of shoots on the same day might require too much organisation, and restricting the event to one or two types is advisable. All the following can be arranged fairly simply.

A *Golf Round* with nine 'holes' made out of small balloons pinned to the turf can be set, with the distances unknown to the players and varying from 20 to 180yd. This is scored as in golf, going round the course twice. '*Poppinloon*' can be improvised whenever helium gas is available, by anchoring a number of balloons floating at the height of a Popinjay roost. The competitors shoot six arrows and count each hit; with the blunt heads and the parachute effect of the flu-fletching it is safe to add the extra amusement of catching the arrows on their way down. '*Splitting the Wand*' is a good test of skill – usually a 2in white strip of plywood at 60yd for men and 3in at 40yd for ladies (quite unnecessary gallantry, here, I should have thought . . .). '*Speed Shooting*' brings one back to the days of Agincourt. In this contest archers try to shoot as many scoring arrows as possible at 30yd in 30sec. (The $2\frac{1}{2}$-min-per-three-arrow-boys will turn puce at the mere mention of this barbaric game!) '*Dartchery*' is scored on a full 4ft replica of a dartboard at 15yd and scored in the same way. Two teams of archers can play or a local darts team can be challenged. Several versions of '*Archery Cricket*' are played. A simple form consists of shooting at three painted stumps on a paper face: each member from the two teams picks a number from a hat, one arrow is shot in turn by each side and when the three stumps have been hit by a team, number one opponent drops out, and so on until one team has been eliminated. Shooting at *Moving Targets* is excitingly refreshing, but, although no blood needs to be spilled, the difficulties involved in making these sometime ingenious contraptions unfortunately restrict this sport to clubs with private grounds. Finally, as a preparation for winter field archery, one can set up a '*Mini-Field Course*' with usual target bosses and small animal faces. The targets are laid out in a semicircle at varying distances from the shooting stake, whose position or that of the targets is changed for each event. Archers shoot singly and the number of arrows making up a round can vary according to the number of targets and archers involved.

During the winter months a number of archers will prefer to give archery a rest. The others will continue with target archery, outdoor or indoor if they are lucky, or will take to field archery. But again, an occasional break from routine will bring back renewed vigour, and this is just what *Roving* (a kind of 'natural golf' where you aim at any suitable marks in open fields), or *Clout Shooting* will do.

Now, if your wife complains that you have forsaken her for archery, you will simply have to make an archer out of her. One problem, though: who will cook Sunday lunch?

3 Equipment

There are still a number of 'bare-bow' clubs in England whose members only use longbows and wooden arrows. They preserve the true grace and skill of early archery, and there is no doubt that from learning to shoot with the traditional longbow and without the various crutches of technology, one can derive incomparable pleasure. However, the flatter trajectory given by modern bows, the more evenly matched metal arrows and the greater safety of practically unbreakable materials have pushed wooden tackle almost out of competitive archery. Unless you can join one of the bare-bow societies or decide to do Field Archery in the longbow class, the making or buying of wooden tackle will be a waste. Even for children, cheap fibreglass bows and alloy arrows are better and safer. As for the making of composite bows by individuals, this is the province of a very small minority of archers. The skilful craftsman who wishes to 'have a go' will be able to buy instruction manuals from archery dealers.

Buying Equipment

'Thus a shooter muste begyn not at the makynge of hys bowe like a bowyer, but at the buynge of hys bowe lyke an archere.' The best advice one can give to a would-be-archer is: WAIT! Rushing to the local sports shop because you have decided to take up archery can be a complete waste of money. You will not really know what your individual requirements or ambitions are and it is very likely that the shop assistant will not know either. It is a sad thing to see a proud novice turn up with a 40lb wooden practice bow which he cannot draw and an expensive set of championship arrows which do not match the bow. He probably needed a 28lb bow and cheap arrows. Incidentally, it would make for less disappointment if the small sports shops (and even a few of the big ones) could send one of their staff to an archery course to enable them to give practical advice.

So, step number one: find where the nearest archery club is, and shoot with them for a few weeks without buying anything (except for a leather tab which will only increase your overdraft by a dollar or a few shillings). Most open clubs have equipment for beginners and are only too glad to lend it to prospective members. All clubs have archers experienced enough to teach you the basic technique and to advise you on buying tackle. On the other hand, it is not really fair to

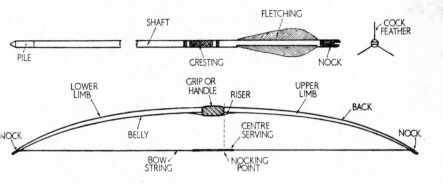

Fig 2. Parts of bow and arrow

go on using club equipment for too long, as it will be needed for other newcomers. After about three weeks' practice, you and your instructor will know what suits your present physical requirements – and your pocket. Specialist archery shops will also be qualified to tell you your needs and they are usually honest enough to discourage beginners from overspending. At the time of writing the cost of a beginner's gear, comprising fibreglass bow, arrows, tab, bracer and ground-quiver, would amount to approximately £14. However, the object of this book is to inform the reader before he takes the plunge. The following pages will give you a detailed account of what an archer must have at the various phases of his progress.

Acquiring tackle can be divided into three stages.

Stage One: first three to six months

Targets

These are one of the many reasons you should join a club, for they cost around £10 each; but you can, of course, buy a small 48in or 24in boss suitable for practice in your garden. There is at the moment only one British firm who makes decent and lasting targets. *Target Stands* are so easy to make that it is really extravagant to buy them (see fig 1, p 11).

Bows

The solid fibreglass bows are undoubtedly the best for beginners.

Three ways of bracing a bow . . .

They are cheap, practically indestructable and will not lose their cast for years; and being so suitable they are very easy to sell when the time comes to buy a more powerful bow. In our experience, they have one small weakness: the arrow shelf is hard on the flights and soon begins to wear out. It is best to fit a flexi-rest right away.

The recommended draw-weight is 24 to 26 lb for ladies, and 26 to 28lb for men. It is useful to remember that the weight stated is for the maximum draw-length (usually 26in or 28in) and that you lose approximately 2lb per inch. When using 27in arrows with a bow marked 28lb at 28in, you will in fact be pulling only 26lb.

As it takes some time to find the maximum draw-weight you can pull comfortably, it is advisable to use club bows for two or three weeks before buying your own. A flat fibreglass will serve you well up to 40 or 50yd, but the recurve bow will pack more punch for the same weight. Although the latter type costs a little more, it is preferable to buy one at the beginning, especially adults, who will want to reach 80yd range. As these bows have 'windows', you must state whether right or left-hander when ordering.

. . . and a fourth

Arrows

Wooden arrows break and their nocks are often too wide for modern bowstrings. Tubular metal arrows are sold in sets of eight and the cheapest will do for the early stages. Clubs or individuals will buy them off you when you get your next set.

It is not much use at this stage to be too particular about your own draw-length, because this will change as you progress. What matters now is a safe length. Should your arrow be too short you could overdraw and hurt your hand or get the arrow stuck in your bow and frighten the life out of your neighbours on the shooting line. An easy safety check consists in placing the nock end of the arrow on the middle of the archer's chest, level with his shoulders, and stretching out the arms, while keeping the shoulders straight, so that the two hands close on the pile of the arrow; at least one inch of arrow should then protrude beyond the fingers. (NB. This method is not accurate enough to ascertain the arrow length for a composite bow.)

A useful guide for beginners' arrows is 28in for men and 26in for ladies and youngsters, bearing in mind that very tall people may need 29in or 30in, specially if they forget to draw to the centre of the chin and slip their anchor point to the side of the face.

More safety precautions against overdrawing will be found in the next chapter.

Bracer or Arm-guard

Briefly, a piece of leather which protects the forearm from the bowstring. A good bracer should have a built-in spine, be easy to put on and comfortable to wear. There are many types available on the market – large and small, thick and thin – in various materials, with three or two straps fitted with press-fasteners, buckles or Velcro; and some with 'easy to fit' elastic which make a farce of bracers, as you must have an arm to fit the bracer instead of the other way round. When you have mislaid your bracer, a pencil and two elastic bands will do.

Beginners should definitely wear a bracer; for most people will, at one time or another, allow their arms to get in the way of the string, and the result, although not dangerous, can be very painful and off-putting. Women are especially vulnerable because of what doctors laughingly call the 'shopping elbow'.

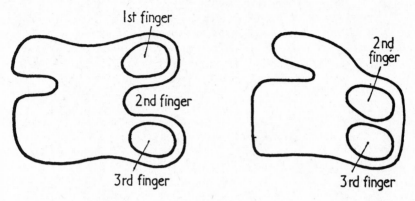

Fig 3. Two widely used tabs

If you do hit your arm above the bracer, don't keep a shameful silence about it; you are doing something drastically wrong, which must be cured immediately. But as the mere mention of 'arm-guard' suggests that you could get hurt, it might not be amiss to go beyond the limits of this chapter and mention one point: with the correct technique you will not only not hit your arm, you won't even touch the bracer. This was laid down in 1545 by our friend Roger Ascham: '. . . but it is best by my iudgemente to give the bowe so much bent that the strynge neede never touche a mannes arme, and so a man neede no bracer, as I knowe manye good archers, whyche occypye none'. There is more to it than a properly braced bow, of course, but we shall talk about it later.

Tab

This piece of smooth leather fits inside your drawing hand and has two purposes: (a) to protect your fingers against the string, and (b) to ensure a clean release, as the fleshy part of your drawing fingers tends to hold on to the string.

There are three main designs to suit archers' theories or style (see fig 3). Tab B is recommended by many coaches as it allows the first finger to feel the position of the hand under the chin (anchor point). Tabs can be made or bought with a double thickness for extra-sensitive fingers or for use with very strong bows. Bought tabs usually have to be cut to fit in with the width of your hand, length of fingers and often to make more room for the arrow nock. Tabs without

Taking the string

finger separators should be kept flat when not in use, perhaps in a wallet or some other convenient place. When shooting, many archers keep their tabs smooth and dry with talcum powder or french chalk.

The traditional material for this vital item was, until recently, leather; but now they are available in Corfam, a material which will not soften in wet weather, and is supposed to be harder wearing. Time will tell. As a matter of interest, if you have an urge to use real bows and arrows under water, you can make your own tab from the plastic lids of coffee tins.

Shooting Glove

This is an alternative to the tab. It offers two main advantages, which might appear to contradict each other: while the fingers are generally better protected, the use of a glove nonetheless gives a far better feeling of the finger-pressure on the bow string and of the position of your anchor point, thus improving the delicate balance of the work done by the drawing hand. A 'keeper' must be worn to prevent the glove from slipping. If you are going to invest in a shooting glove, buy the best, for a bad glove will ruin your release. It may also be a good idea to buy one on the tight side as it may stretch. What is sometimes called a 'skeleton glove', a mere extension of the keeper, with thick cone-like pieces of hard leather, takes ages to break in. These are less than half the price of proper gloves, but are, in my opinion, useless.

Quiver

It will keep your arrows together and within convenient reach of your hand while you shoot. The simple method of sticking your arrows in the ground in front of you was all right at Agincourt, but strictly against FITA rules!

There are four kinds of quiver, starting with the 'ground quiver', which is but a slight improvement on medieval times. Instead of pushing your six missiles into the turf, you drive in a spike fitted with one little guard that keeps the arrows vertical without one's having to push them into the ground; but the word 'quiver' in 'ground quiver' is really a misnomer, for it is generally used purely as a bow-stand. Two kinds of archers will use it: beginners without complete equipment, to prevent their arrows from being trodden on, and

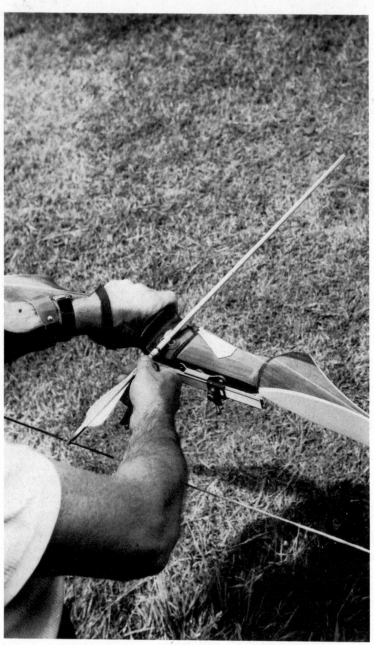

Nocking the arrow

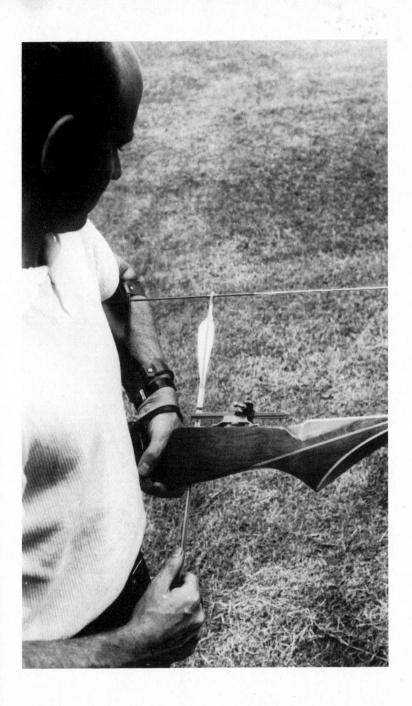

others, to rest their bows on — for this purpose a ground quiver is indispensable. Indeed, the serious beginner should certainly acquire one, as his bow could be damaged by careless feet or dampness. The other quivers are dealt with on page 30.

Bowstring

Even the new archer would be well advised to carry a spare string. Experienced archers are never without one. They should be replaced at the first sign of fraying, as a string liable to break can be dangerous. Bowstrings can be made at home, if you have time; or you can get one by return of post from your archery dealer. Dacron is now widely used and easily available. No matter what you are told, Dacron strings need treating with beeswax to keep the moisture out.

Dental Floss

This is wound round the serving of the string to mark the exact spot where the arrow should be nocked.

Nocking Point

Dental floss is wound above, below or on both sides of this spot, or on the nocking point itself if the bowstring is not quite thick enough for the arrow nock. (An arrow, once nocked on the bowstring should not fall if pointed vertically at the ground, but should come off at the flick of a finger.)

Bowsight

All you need now is a homemade device costing a few pence, eg a strip of foam draught-excluder stuck on the back of the bow and a colour-headed pin. For a few pence more you can cut a length of plastic curtain runner and use the eye screw as a movable sight.

Stage Two

You have now been shooting for three to six months, you have mastered the basic standard technique, your style is no longer erratic and your muscles are well tuned. If you have a flat bow, or if you feel much stronger than when you started, you will want something more powerful, something to give you a flatter cast at the long distances; and if you are absolutely sure that archery is going to be your sport

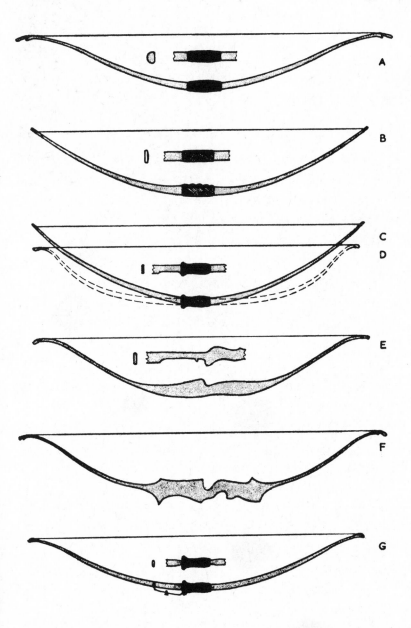

Fig 4. Bows used in modern archery: A. Longbow (yew); B. Practice or flat bow (lemonwood); C and D. Fibreglass bows, flat and recurve; E. Composite bow (fibreglass, wood, plastic); F. Composite bow, weight-stabilised; G. Tubular steel bow fitted with metal sight

(or one of your sports), you might invest in a composite bow (see STAGE THREE). On the other hand, with a recurve and heavier fibreglass, there is no real need for a composite yet. A season with another glass bow would allow you to settle into your maximum draw-weight, find your exact length of arrow, and help you to acquire that final confidence necessary to use expensive equipment.

Draw-weight for the second bow should be roughly 36lb for men and 28lb for ladies, remembering that when your draw-length is shorter than the bow's maximum draw, you are not in fact pulling the full weight. Here again, it is unwise to buy without consulting a coach or one of the big dealers.

Quivers

Belt Quivers are purely for arrows, though you can buy them fitted with little pockets for score books, pencils, etc. They come in different shapes and sizes, the most popular being the flat 'fan' type, simple in design and with the advantage of keeping flights apart; it also offers convenient space for your club insignia. The very cheap ones will save you nothing, as you will soon grow irritated by the rattling of arrows within, and the dropping of arrows every time you bend down. If you are handy with leather and wood, quivers are fairly easy to make at home and can bring a touch of individuality to your tackle.

Pocket Quivers, although a little casual in appearance have the advantage of being less than a third of the price of the conventional quiver. It is simply an inner pocket made to fit inside your own hip pocket – definitely not for ladies!

Shoulder Quivers are for field archery only; with one or two straps, and with or without knife, they fill their role both aesthetically and practically when shooting in rough country, but would be quite out of place for target archery.

Pipe Quivers really do exist. They hold a pipe very conveniently on your belt and can make splendid birthday or Christmas presents.

Arrows

They should now be stiffer and better matched, which means buying the next grade in quality and expense. (Clubs or beginners will probably buy your old set.)

Sights

At this stage, most archers feel that a pin and draught-excluder isn't good enough. Of course, it is still perfectly adequate; in fact, you can reach very high standards with it. But a proper sight gives more pleasure and looks much better. For glass bows you can buy a fairly cheap nylon or plastic track which can be glued to the back of the bow, usually supplied with both pin and ring sights.

Score Book

When you start shooting the rounds such a book becomes necessary, and the psychological value of keeping scores and comparing the old and new is undeniable. In archery, one competes mostly against oneself; every improvement is a victory, and when you feel somewhat depressed about your current shooting, flick through the pages of your score book and see how much worse you were a few months or a year ago! There is no need to shoot complete Rounds to keep score — comparing your best dozen at each distance is a good way to check your progress.

Stage Three

Composite Bow

Now you want to shoot good scores at 80 and 100yd and take part in matches and tournaments and so off you go to choose your composite bow. What guidance do you need? Three factors should be taken into account when buying a bow which will give you the maximum cast for your physical characteristics: your draw-length, your own strength and the distance between your eyes and your anchor point.

It is now vitally important to measure your exact draw-length, taken, naturally, at full draw with your bow arm fully extended (but not locked) and the string touching the middle of your chin. A quarter of an inch protruding beyond the arrow rest isn't a bad thing, but no more. (The width between the arrow rest and the belly of a composite is greater than with practice bows and reduces the risk of dangerously overdrawing almost to nothing (see fig 4).)

The draw-length is measured between the nock and the pile of the arrow (see fig 2).

Having established your arrow length, you must now work out the

Full draw

The loose

length and the weight of bow which will give you the maximum and flattest cast. Weight for weight and length for length, this will vary with the archer's physiognomy: a man with a round face or small chin will have to aim higher than the handsome chap with a Greek profile. It is a good precaution to ask a friend with your draw-length to let you try his bow, which you must do *without altering his sight*. If you shoot consistently higher than he does, you obviously will get better performance from the same bow; but if you keep low on the target, you will need a stronger or shorter bow. For instance, if a 66in bow at 36lb doesn't give you a sight mark at 100yd, you will need a 64in or even 62in bow. Forty yards is enough to find this out, and it saves walking.

Remember also the 2lb loss per inch of arrow. With that 36lb at 28in, you will only be drawing 34lb with your 27in arrows or 32lb with a 26in shaft. Of course, short arrows are lighter than long ones and fly further. But first we must settle the question of your composite bow.

As a rough guide, we can say that 66in bows are suitable for 28in draw-lengths, 64in for 27in and 62in for 26in and under. It must also be considered that the shorter the bow the less smooth its action and the easier it is to pinch the arrow (because of the sharper angle of the string at full draw).

Composite bows come in a variety of designs and in two distinct groups: stabilised and non-stabilised (see fig 4). Stabilised bows have extra weight to reduce vibration and sideways movement on release. If you can afford the additional cost, they are definitely worth it. Your choice of composite will also be influenced by its actual weight (weight in hand), by the size and shape of the handle and, of course, by its looks. Browsing through archery catalogues and trying to choose one of the forty American, British and Japanese bows available can provide a few enjoyable evenings. Once you have decided, it is wise to go to the dealers or bowyers to make quite sure that the bow feels right to handle and to draw. Watch out for bows that 'stack', or suddenly become harder to pull before full draw.

In short, maximum performance and aesthetic pleasure are what you are looking for, though you must remember that it is the man behind the equipment that counts. Very costly equipment doesn't automatically mean good results; you stand just as good a chance of

becoming a Grand Master Bowman with a fairly cheap bow as with a
lavish job fitted with the latest gimmicks.

Arrows

Your ambition is now not simply to hit the target but to group your
shots as tightly as possible. For this it is necessary to have arrows
carefully matched in weight and with a degree of stiffness that exactly
suits the bow. (The main countries manufacturing arrows are Britain,
the USA and Sweden; they sometimes combine, eg American shafts,
Swedish nocks, etc.)

The weight of an arrow is not only governed by its length but also
by its wall thickness and diameter, wall thickness combined with
length of shaft giving the arrow its particular degree of stiffness (spine
rating). Now, why is correct spine so important to good shooting?
This is where the so-called 'archer's paradox' comes in. During its
violent departure from the bow, the arrow is made to curve on the
side of the bow by an outward movement of the drawing hand. It
first bends outwards, then springs back inwards just as the flights clear
the handle, and this snaking motion goes on with diminishing
strength for as much as 30yd. This is why an arrow shot at a short
distance with a strong bow sometimes looks as if it had been shot
from quite a different place on the shooting line, and why consistent
shooting at short ranges eventually bends your arrows. With modern
bows and their cut-away windows, the reaction is less violent than
with longbows, but even with sight windows cut past centre there is
still a noticeable springing in and out – a reaction which, if
exaggerated by too stiff or too whippy an arrow, will obviously cause
trouble. A well behaved arrow is one that doesn't give a parting kick
to the bow. As your curiosity may be aroused, perhaps I should
explain how the stiffness of an arrow is measured. The British method
is by applying $1\frac{1}{2}$lb pressure on the centre of the arrow while both
ends are supported. The bending is taken to 1/100th of an inch. A
fairly stiff arrow, rated as 50 spine will show a deflection of $\frac{1}{2}$in. The
higher the spine rating, the more supple the arrow. The weight is
measured in grains, and so, we could have 26in arrows with the
following characteristics: 263/66 for a 28lb bow or 285/53 at 36lb.

Scientifically minded archers can talk endlessly about
spine/weight/length/draw-weight ratio. Personally, the thought that

The draw, back view. Composite bow with twin stabilisers and clicker; closed hand grip. The archer is leaning a little too far back for the distance at which he is shooting, hence sloping shoulder line and raised elbow

I was shooting with a quiverful of 24SRT-X, 1913 271/520 would kill the romance of archery stone dead. Let us take comfort in the knowledge that reputable archery shops are like good osteopaths: they will solve your spine troubles. If after that, you still do not shoot straight, you'd better start working on your technique.

Arrow Fletching

There are now two types of fletchings: feathers and plastic. The main idea of fletchings is to keep the arrow on a straight and steady course. To ensure an even straighter flight, spin must be imparted. Feathers, having a rough and a smooth side, will therefore have more air friction on one side than on the other (provided the feathers come from *the same wing*) and thus create a spin. As the spinning of the arrow creates drag, the arrow-maker is again confronted with a delicate balance: too much spin would reduce the cast. Plastic vanes, creating no uneven air friction, have to be offset to impart spin.

The length of the vanes will depend on the type of archery practised: it may vary from 2in for target archery to $4\frac{1}{2}$in for hunting arrows. Feathers look and feel 'right' and they don't react dangerously to faulty technique. Plastic vanes are lighter, more uniform in weight, and unaffected by rain or humidity; most top archers seem to prefer them, but they are merciless on faulty technique – a bad loose will rip them off the shaft or even cut you.

Four-fletched arrows are meant to fly straighter and to allow smaller vanes, but experts disagree on their alleged advantages.

Fletching Jig

Sooner or later, flights will get damaged and a jig will help you to glue new vanes on your arrows in the correct position. Fletching jigs vary greatly in price and intricacy, but even the simplest and cheapest will be found useful by the average archer.

Arrow Straightening Aids

These can be of great value in a club, where many beginners' arrows will glance off the target stands, but they are rather expensive for private use. Such aids do not straighten your bent arrows – you do! They help by showing you exactly where to exert pressure and, most important, when to stop.

Bowstrings

If you shoot often you will need three strings a year. No real archer will ever be without a spare string. Experts vary in their preferences for material and thickness. Thick strings are supposed to shoot straighter, and thin strings further, but the width of your arrow nocks must be considered. The usual thickness for Dacron B strings is 10 to 14 strands for a 36lb bow. All strings for the composite and adult fibreglass bows are double-looped. The one-loop strings, which have to be secured at the other end with a timber hitch, are only used for children's bows and self bows (made of one piece of wood).

A small, useful job which you should be able to do is to replace the serving on your bowstring, either by hand or with the help of a 'serving tool'. The server requires a certain amount of dexterity. All 'aids' are just that: aids. No matter how much you pay, the notion that you can buy a wonderful gadget which will do all the work is a fallacy.

Serving should be started 2in above the nocking point and continued downwards for about 6in. The purpose of serving the string is to prevent fraying upon repeated contact with the bracer; it also makes it a little less hard on the fingers.

Bracing Height Gauge

This useful gadget helps you to check the distance between the string and the belly or the back of the bow. It also locates the proper place for the nocking point. More about 'Bracing Height' will be found in the next chapter.

Bowsights

Although you can spend some £15 or so on a bowsight, it must be emphasised that expensive sights are a waste of money unless your technique gives you at least 99 per cent consistency. Why spend a fortune for a masterpiece of engineering, giving elevation adjustment up to .0015in, when you are liable to 'pluck' your string and hit a white at 11 o'clock? A foot moved a couple of inches on the shooting line, a jaw more clenched or relaxed than usual, a rigid knee or whimsical breeze, all this will affect your grouping. I have known archers develop some minor fault of technique and blame their bad shooting on their intricate sights, adjusting and readjusting with mounting irritation until they have missed the target altogether. Stick to simple sights until every point of shooting becomes automatic.

For the best sight mark, the sight should be fixed to the belly of the bow. Simply glueing on the track is a waste of time; screw it on, drilling a slightly bigger hole in the fibreglass to avoid splitting.

Bowcase

A good composite bow is like a thoroughbred – tremendously strong but very vulnerable – and a deep scratch in the fibreglass can ruin it. Hence the absolute necessity for a bowcase. They usually have a soft lining and are made of vinyl, with or without handles or pockets.

Bowsling

This reassures archers using the 'open-hand grip' (surely a contradiction in terms). It is a simple leather strap fixed to the bow handle and round your wrist. Secure in the thought that your bow won't fall to the ground on release, you then have no excuse for the last-second fatal 'grab'.

Equipment Cases

These neat boxes have racks for one or two sets of arrows and room for all the other odds and ends, like quivers, sights, spare strings, etc. The advantages to the serious archer are obvious. Unfortunately they are rather costly, but many archers make their own.

Folding Chair

Light and small to carry, it can make all the difference in tournaments. No matter how fit you are, standing from 10 am to 6 pm can be pretty tiring. And, of course, you don't just stand. Shooting a 'York Round' you would be walking 4,800yd, nearly $2\frac{3}{4}$ miles – not counting the frantic rush for a pub during the lunch break. . . .

Field Glasses

They help to spot your shots and correct your aiming. However, you need really good ones if you are to recognise your nocks and fletchings. They are used mostly in tournaments, though many good archers dispense with them altogether.

Footmarkers

Large flat drawing-pins can be used to stick in the turf to mark the position of your feet on the shooting line. Golf tees are often used, but tend to bury themselves in the ground.

Optional Equipment

The following items may or may not be necessary for the good archer. One item will be considered vital by some and as a mere gimmick by others. There is a real danger in becoming more interested in the gadgets than in the sport, whether it be ski-ing, sailing, fishing or archery. Activities, of which the enjoyment depends so much on one's own guts and brains, are bound to lose their magic with the use of scientific aids. The enjoyment of archery is an intricate lacework of primitive, aesthetic and spiritual fibres. The chap who screws a long poker stabiliser on to his bow may add a few points to his score, but certainly nothing to the beauty of archery. However, you will not know whether a particular device may suit your needs until you have tried it.

Clickers (or klickers). Almost every bow displayed at tournaments is fitted with a clicker. This device is usually made of a thin strip of springy metal through which you thread the arrow. When the arrow has been drawn to its full length, the clicker snaps back onto the bow and thus gives the signal: click! There is no point in being too facetious about it, because many excellent archers use it. However, even the makers themselves state that it should be used only to cure inconsistent draw-length or 'gold shyness' (see Chapter 4) and then abandoned. Coaches, with friendly dealers and manufacturers in mind, are noncommital at first, but, when pressed, they will assure you that perfectly consistent draw-length can be achieved with proper practice and technique, as obviously it should be.

External Stabilisers are another American invention meant to help the archer to improve his score (fig 5). The long or short pokers fitted on the back of the bow reduce movement and vibration, but tend to make the lover of beauty shudder. It is interesting to note that the British are, as usual, going wild over an innovation just at the time when its country of origin is beginning to discard it. A leading American bowyer is returning to an absence of ironmongery, but retaining maximum stabilisation with a new heavy material in the handle.

A good anchor

Holding and follow-through . . .

. . . perfect steadiness in both actions

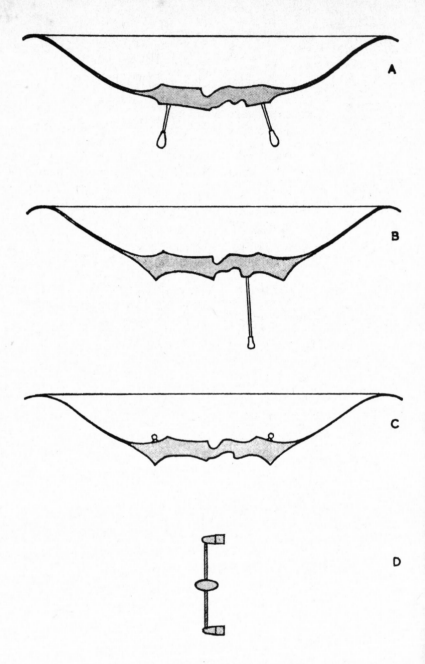

Fig 5. External stabilisers: A. Twin; B. Mono; C. Ball; D. Outrigged.

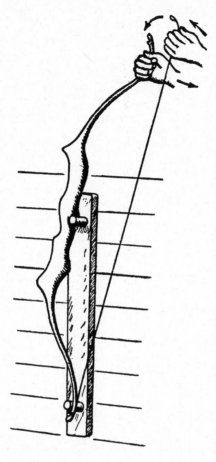

Fig 6. Bow-stringer for club hut – two pieces of broomstick with foam rubber

Bowstringers. There is only one proper way to brace (or string) a composite bow; but, if you have ever pulled a ligament in your back, it is the wrong way! Many archers use the step-through method, which is much less strenuous but risks twisting the bow limbs. So, naturally, bowstringers are being manufactured, some simple and not too expensive, and others beautiful, cumbersome and far too dear, considering that a small length of rope will do just as well. You could also fit a home-made bowstringer outside the club house, using two bits of broomstick and foam rubber (see fig 6).

String Keepers. They should prevent the string slipping off the bow

Follow-through, open-hand grip, mono-stabiliser

when the latter is unstrung. Some people find it useful but most pronounce it a confounded nuisance, specially if the loops of the strings are narrow ones.

Nocklocks. Amusing at first, discarded later. They are little bits of rubber threaded on to the string to position the nocking point. By using six instead of two, you can apparently dispense with a tab. They tend to reduce cast and deaden the all important feel of finger pressure on the string. Anyone who buys them (at $22\frac{1}{2}$p or around 60 cents a pair) has money to throw away.

Brushnocks. They are meant to prevent small branches catching in the string while hunting. If you have a 'noisy bow' they will cushion the impact of the string against the bow limbs and quieten that unnerving twang. But they also reduce the cast: and, more often than not, a 'noisy bow' denotes faults in technique, not in equipment.

One could also talk of hand-warmers and adjustable umbrellas, powder pouches and hand-locaters, flu-flies and fur fletchings – but it is time to consider the last important item on our list.

Clothing

There is no need, at first, to spend anything. The two points to remember are to avoid wearing loose garments or gaudy colours. Very thick 'floppy' sweaters and some wide-sleeved shirts will catch the string. When the weather is cold, it is better to wear several thin layers. (Quilted anoraks are out!) Later on, when you have shot for a few weeks and feel like an archer, you may want to look the part.

One of the prime characteristics of archery is quietness: nothing must offend the ears or the eyes! But quietness should by no means be equated with dullness. Lady archers can look ravishing in white, or white and green, and a whole line of men in dark green tops and white or fawn trousers makes a pleasant sight. There is no reason why one should feel self-conscious at wearing a 'uniform', any more than cricketers or tennis players should when wearing the same colour clothes. Clubs can bring a touch of individuality with badges, head-gears and tassels. Of course, when the rains come down and gales howl, conventions are often swept aside – anything that keeps you dry and does not impede your shooting will do – but even then, it is still possible to wear waterproof clothes of suitable colours.

4 Shooting

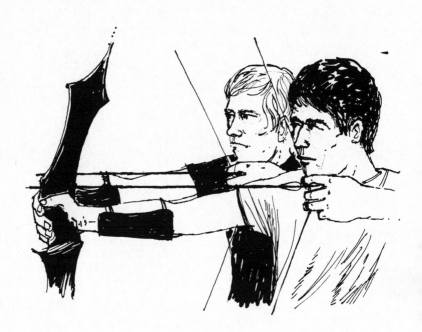

Where and When

Beginners practise on ranges varying from 10 to 30yd. With the 20yd needed behind the target, this means a pretty big lawn. If this area is not available, a wall of straw bales or a (very expensive) archery net will be required. Arrows landing in your neighbour's garden or greenhouse would not serve the cause of archery nor enhance friendly relationships.

The other prerequisite besides space is closely cut grass. Nothing is more infuriating than wasting hours searching for lost arrows, and a two-inch growth can so hide your precious shaft that you will not find it until the mowing machine makes mincemeat of it.

But even if you are lucky enough to own a suitable lawn no real archer will forever shoot at 30 or even 60yd, nor will he remain satisfied shooting by himself; hence the need to join a club. GNAS regional secretaries, or the NAA, will give you a list of clubs in your area, and your local sports dealer may also be able to inform you (see Chapter 5). Later, when you and your friends feel experienced enough, you may find it desirable to form your own society. This is an exciting challenge (see also Chapter 5).

The shooting season varies with the whims of the climate, but in Britain outdoor target archery officially starts in May and goes on till late September. Most clubs practise two or three times a week on the average – at weekends and one evening during the week. Some hardy maniacs will bend their bows when ski-ing would be more advisable, but in fact archery on skis is practised in Austria and Japan, and given enough snow, there is no reason why we should not have a go ourselves.

In the winter, beside the unstoppable archers who will shoot the long distances out of doors, there are the lucky clubs who have found an indoor range (old wartime huts, riding schools, airfield hangars, etc). Enterprising clubs with friends in the right places should never have to stop shooting, though occasional bouts of archery indigestion and family holidays will sometimes interfere with practice for short periods of time.

Field archery usually runs from late autumn to early spring. Although a pale imitation of field archery can take place on recreation grounds, the real thing should be done in a wooded area with dales and hillocks.

Learning the draw: fingers on string and position of drawing-arm. Practice fibreglass bow; strip of draught excluder for pin-sight

How

How pleasant it would be to teach a sport without having to use the word 'technique'. Anything less graceful, more unbending and less romantic is difficult to imagine. 'Technique' pricks the poet's flesh; it is completely alien to the thrills of primitive enjoyment. But any joy that demands skill requires practice, and practice is useless without the knowing-how-to-do-it-in-the-best-most-efficient-and-most-effortless-way, fourteen words that can be boiled into one: 'technique'. There will always be the right and the wrong ways of doing anything; and, in the middle, is a subtle range of 'wrong' ways that suit some people, and 'right' ways that stifle others. However, when starting a sport, it is better to follow a method offering the maximum of efficiency and simplicity. It is with this in mind that the GNAS coaches have evolved what they call the 'standard technique' for target archery.

While much can be learnt from a book, one must stress the fact that help from experienced friends or instructors is essential in the early stages, and also later, when you cannot pinpoint that infuriating new fault.

Standard Technique

Safety

After the various parts of your equipment have been described and their use made clear, a few words must be mentioned about the all-important subject of *safety*. It is perhaps because archery is such a lethal sport that one never hears of a serious accident. Carelessness, exceptional clumsiness or youthful ragging are simply not allowed. The following rules for your own safety, and for the safety of others, should be clearly understood before you start shooting:

1. If anyone shouts 'FAST'! stop shooting. (*Fast*, from the expression *stand fast*, don't move.)
2. Do not step forward from the shooting line for *any* reason until everyone has shot his last arrow.
3. Do not shoot from behind the line.
4. Do not draw a wooden bow without an arrow; it might break and damage your face.
5. Draw to the centre of your chin. (This avoids over-drawing and sticking the arrow into your hand or your bow.)

6. If you do overdraw and the arrow is jammed into the bow handle, *do not panic.* Simply lean forward from the waist and go on pulling.
7. For the same reason, do not shoot with too short arrows.
8. When bracing the bow, make sure the loops of the string are fully engaged in the bow nocks; also keep your face well away, as a bow that slips and springs back can hit you in the eye.
9. Do not shoot with frayed strings *or* broken flights.
10. In the very early stages, make sure you are not placing the arrow on the wrong side of the bow, or it will fly off at a wide angle.
11. Never shoot an arrow straight up in the air: it might come down on to and through somebody's head, perhaps yours.

Dominant Eye

There are several ways of checking which of your eyes is the dominant one. A friend can do this for you. He should cover one of his eyes and ask you to point at his uncovered eye with one finger, then repeat with your other hand. Both times your fingers will come in line under your dominant eye. This test can also be done by holding out a ring in the fingers of your two hands, with outstretched arms, and looking at your friend's uncovered eye through the ring; the latter will come directly under your dominant eye.

If you are right-eyed and right-handed, you have a good start. You can shoot with both eyes open or with the left one shut, as you like; shooting with both eyes open is an advantage at long distances. If your dominant eye is the left one, you should try shooting left-handed. Many left-eyed right-handers in fact eventually adapt the angle of their heads and their 'windows' to cope with the situation. A right-handed archer with *no* dominant eye *must* close his left eye.

Bracing the Bow

There are three ways of bracing (or stringing) the bow. These are explained for a right-handed archer, and left-handers will reverse the method.

(*a*) Rest the end of the bow, with the loop engaged in the nock, against your right instep. Hold the bow with the right hand round

Junior learning the draw. Fibreglass bow, two kinds of quiver

the *handle* and pull, while, with the left hand, you *push* the upper loop and the upper limb simultaneously with the thumb and forefinger until the loop is securely in the nock. Bracing the bow feels awkward and difficult at first, but is a knack very quickly acquired. This first method can be used with all bows but requires strength and know-how with heavy composite bows.

(*b*) The 'step-through' method can be used with old steel bows, recurve fibreglass and composite bows. Provided care is taken not to twist the limbs of composite bows, this way is easier for the archer. The left leg goes between the bow and the string (string uppermost). The lower recurve of the bow rests against the front of the right ankle, and the belly of the bow is brought against the left hip as far as possible behind the archer. While his left hand pushes the upper limb forward, his right hand engages the loop of the string in the nock. This method is frowned upon by the authorities, but it is better than pulling all the ligaments in your back.

(*c*) Bowstringers have a dual purpose: they make it easier to brace the bow and eliminate the risks of twisting the limbs. There are two models on the market, but a very simple and efficient one can be made with a short length of rope tied into a loop. The lower nock should rest on some soft, clean material — a discarded rubber rest from a car roof-rack is ideal. Another homemade device suitable for clubs, which can be fixed on the wall of the club hut, simply consists of two bits of broomstick wrapped in foam rubber (see fig 6, p 43).

Placing the Sight

You will probably start shooting at 20yd. For this distance, a rough guide for the position of the sighting pin is the length between the archer's eye and his chin plus one finger's width. Measure this from the arrow rest upwards and stick the pin on the back of the bow. For the first dozen arrows or so, just be content to hit the target. When you stop shaking and can draw a constant length, adjust the pin if necessary. Bring it down if you shoot too low, bring it up if you shoot too high, pull it out if you are shooting left and push it in if you are going right.

Position on the Shooting Line

The right-handed archer, like the golfer, points his left shoulder towards his mark. First, you should place your feet astride the shooting line, with your head up and looking down the line. The feet should be spaced shoulder width apart (not too wide, to avoid stiffness, and not too close, to preserve balance). While still looking down the line, raise your left arm and point where you think the target is; then turn your head and look at the target. If your arm is pointing to the right or left of it, adjust your position by moving the angle of your feet until shoulders, arms and feet are all in one line, pointing at the centre of the target. The alignment should *not* be achieved by twisting the hips.

Recap: Feet astride the line – head up – relax – check alignment.

Holding the Bow

A bow should be held lightly and never 'gripped'. The following routine will help the beginner to acquire the correct hand position. (*a*) With your left hand hanging relaxed at your side, hold the bow by the handle, string upwards resting against and inside your arm. (*b*) Stretch your thumb so that it is in line with the upper limb. This gives you the correct position for the hand round the handle. (If the wrist is cocked inside the bow you will hit your arm; if it is cocked outwards, strain and jerkiness will result.) *(c)* With the arm straight, bring the bow level with the shoulder and horizontal. *(d)* Turn your wrist anticlockwise until the bow is vertical. There should be ample clearance between the bowstring and your bracer. If there isn't, repeat the whole process from scratch, checking that the fleshy part of the thumb isn't too far in. Hold *lightly*. The bow will be held in place by the push/pull action of the draw.

Nocking the Arrow

You may remember that the spot where the arrow is nocked on the string should be at a right-angle to the arrow rest or $\frac{1}{8}$in above that point.

1st method (preferable for beginners): Hold the bow horizontally, about waist high. Without touching the flights of the arrow, place it on the bow (careless beginners holding the bow vertical, sometimes place the arrow on the wrong side – left for right-handers. This mistake will not occur if the bow is held horizontal). With the arrow resting on the arrow shelf or rest, pull it back to engage the nock into the nocking point. From this moment it is no longer necessary to hold or touch any part of the arrow with either hand. (Once nocked, the arrow should not fall off if pointed at the ground, but should come off at the flick of a finger. If it does fall off, a little extra thickness is wanted on the serving.)

2nd method. Hold the bow with arm hanging relaxed by your side, then bring the handle to your hip, allowing the string to touch your forearm. Hold the arrow roughly in the middle of the shaft, pass it under the bow, making sure that the cock feather points away from the bow, and engage the nock on the nocking point. You can now place your fingers on the string and let your arm come down again, ready for the draw. This method is quicker than the first and feels more natural.

Placing the Drawing Hand on the String

The most comfortable place for the string is in the first crease of the fingers. Further in is almost bound to 'foul the loose' and a position nearer the tip of the fingers makes it difficult to hold the string and creates tension. The drawing fingers are the first, second and third.

The first being placed above the arrow and the second and third below it. Care should be taken not to pinch the arrow, specially during the first two or three weeks; always make sure you leave a little free space between fingers and arrow. There is no need to curl the fingers round the string, as the pressure on the tendons will make the first joints bend naturally. At the very beginning a tab may feel a hindrance – it seems to get in the way, making a difficult job even more difficult – and provided your fingers can stand it, there is no harm in shooting without it; but as soon as you have mastered the basic actions of drawing and loosing, you must wear a tab.

Practice Loose

Some beginners, who have practised drawing and aiming and want to shoot their first arrow, find they can't let go of the string! To avoid this embarrassing situation, it is advisable to become aware of what actually happens during the loose. With the arrow still pointing down, push your bow away from you (about hip high), draw the arrow half length (keeping your wrist well in line with your arm), and open your fingers, thus releasing the arrow into the ground. Do this two or three times until the actions seem natural. You are now ready to learn the draw.

Aiming

A good draw looks smooth and easy, but is in fact a complex action, which should include aiming. 'Instinctive aiming', or aiming without a sight, will be described later, it is used in hunting, roving, archery, golf and field archery. In modern target archery a sight is always used and on practice bows a pin is usually placed at the right height by your instructor. When aiming, the pin should be on the Gold, and the bow held quite vertically across the target. It can be useful to become aware of the slight tilt of the head by practising the following checks: with the feet in the right position, stand erect and relaxed, looking down the shooting line; place an arrow with the pile resting on your chest and with its shaft in contact with the middle of your chin and the middle of your nose; then hold the arrow in this position and turn your face until you are looking at the target and can see the arrow vertical across the target. Do this a few times to acquire the feel of the head position (fig 7).

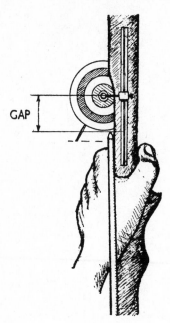

Fig 7. Aiming – alignment

Draw

The bow and bow arm are pointing down; the bow hand is relaxed and correctly positioned round the handle; the three drawing fingers, placed round the nocking point, are gently feeling the pressure of the string; and neither wrist is cocked in any direction. You are ready. Now, simultaneously raise the bow hand until the sight is on the gold *(bow vertical!)*, and bring your drawing hand to the centre of the chin. This must be done with an even push/pull action, applying pressure with your bow hand and pulling the string with the back and shoulder muscles (you must *not* pull with your hand). Feeling imaginary pressure on your drawing elbow will help to use the right muscles. When the draw is completed the string should be in contact with the middle of the chin and the middle of the nose should be allowed to touch the string. Your first finger must be directly under the chin and touching it, the thumb and little finger both being relaxed and kept out of the way. This location of hand fingers and string at full draw is called the *anchor point*.

British coaches advise breathing in with the draw and holding your

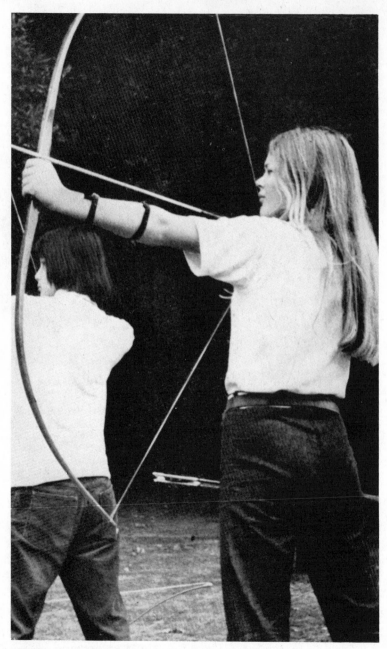

Club practice: a promising junior

breath until after the follow-through. Some American archers use the rifle shooting method of expelling air before the draw and loose.

Practise the draw without an arrow at first. Do not loose without an arrow but comeback to 'neutral' gently. Keep practising until you are reasonably aware of the following points:

1. String touching middle of chin.
2. Nose resting on string (without 'poking').
3. Back of drawing hand relaxed and in line with drawing arm.
4. Drawing elbow level with shoulders and bow arm.
5. Left shoulder out of the way.
6. Bow arm *slightly* bent.
7. Bow hand and fingers relaxed, with bow held mainly by pressure on bowl of thumb.

NOW, place an arrow on your bow, nock it carefully, draw until the string touches your chin; WAIT! Is the string really touching the middle of your chin? Is the pin on the Gold? Right. WAIT! Count at least two seconds, then, while continuing the push/pull action, completely relax the fingers and allow them to come off the string. As your chin is now in the way of the string, the latter cannot move further back and the fingers being drawn back, have to open.

So, you have shot your first arrow. If it is a Gold, it may be beginner's luck, or good shooting; the next five will tell you. If they are all in the Gold, you will soon be wanted by your County Team! But it is more likely that your first shots will be widely spread all over the target. In fact, if you hit the target you should be pleased. There is nothing unusual or shameful about hitting the green at this stage. When you get all your arrows on the target, you can see whether your sight needs adjusting or not. Move it if necessary and keep on practising until you start grouping. Do not be too serious or grim about it; just enjoy yourself and try to feel as relaxed as possible, when you start feeling tired, STOP!

After a few days' practice, muscles which had never been used before become stronger; completely new actions become familiar and with your confidence grows the ambition for consistent and good grouping. For this, a more careful study of technique will be required, starting with the loose.

Loose

The loose or release is certainly the most delicate action in archery. Some beginners achieve the perfect loose very quickly and with a minimum of explanation. Such lucky archers need not read or talk too much about it, but leave well alone. Others have to learn the hard way, or may develop faults without being aware of them. For a good or 'clean' loose, the string is pulled to the centre of the chin with fingers 2 and 3 exerting even pressure and finger 1 merely touching the string. While you check and hold your aim (long enough to make sure everything is all right but not longer than you can manage comfortably) push/pull is maintained with the help of the back muscles until the fingers are allowed to open. They should then stay close to each other, not spread out; and the hand should come a few inches behind the chin as near the neck as possible, and *not* be jerked away from the face. A clean loose will not twist the string on release, but a snatched loose will increase the spine reaction and foul the flight of the arrow. Roger Ascham's apparently perplexing words still remain the best description of the perfect loose: 'Quick and hard so that it might be without twitches, yet soft and gentle that the shaft might fly truly.'

Follow-through

After the loose, the archer should remain rock-solid right to the moment of impact (a nice sharp thump if the arrow hits the target, silence if it hits the green). The only slight movement permissible is a straightening of the bow arm towards the target, seemingly punching the Gold.

String Alignment (Aiming 2)

Many archers, shooting with both eyes open, shoot perfectly straight simply by aiming with their bowsight and maintaining a consistent anchor point.

Archers aiming with one eye closed, however, often use the bowstring as extra check. Normally, the eye cannot focus on both string and sight at once; looking at the string requires conscious effort. When seen, it will appear to be in line with the left-hand side of the bow or, ideally, with the sight; it can also be seen on the right-hand side. The space seen between string and sight is called the window.

Window

The window is said to be 'open' when the space is on the left, and 'closed' when it is on the right. Archers using the string alignment will find where the window should be to suit them, and can mark the spot on the upper limb of the bow. Other ways of using the string for consistency are making another mark (a bit of tape) on the string, in line with the aiming eye, or using a 'kisser' (a bead or tape), which comes in contact with the lips in the same place for each shot.

It must be stressed, however, that people with slight spinal or eye abnormalities will develop their own aiming techniques. For such archers, suddenly becoming aware of the string may completely wreck their shooting.

Grip

There are two distinctive ways of holding the bow: *(a)* with the hand completely closed round the handle; and *(b)* with the four fingers spread out and thumb pressed gently against the handle.

Method *(b)*, or the open-hand grip has obvious advantages. The bow being held mainly by pressure against the bowl of the thumb, there is far less risk of imparting a twist (or torque) on release, and, therefore, less or no chance of window variation. This grip also allows the bow to follow its normal forward impetus on release, giving it its maximum and smoothest cast. When using the open-hand grip, it is advisable to employ a bowsling to prevent the bow from jumping out of your hand, or to curl the first finger round the handle, letting it touch the thumb lightly.

Archers using the closed-hand grip should never vary the tension in their hold. Slight variations will have pronounced torque effect, and an unduly hard grip will reduce the cast and throw the arrow off course. When considering the problems of grips, it must be remembered that the bow *must* move on release; should the arm or the hand be too stiff, the impetus will be sideways instead of forward.

Bringing the Sight on to the Gold (Aiming 3)

The habit of drawing with the drawing unit angled high on the target, bringing your sight gradually down on to the Gold should be discouraged. Beside wasting time and energy it may contribute to the dreaded disease of 'Gold Shyness'. This very real trouble sometimes

Tournament: top archers against the evening sun

afflicts good archers in their first or second years. It is a mixture of physical and psychological tension which results in the archer loosing before his sight reaches the Gold. As the trouble becomes worse, the archer trying to approach the Gold from above or from below, will jerk his bow arm up or down and his style will deteriorate even further. Concerned friends can do little to help; the cure for Gold Shyness is a lonely battle with oneself, but one which the true archer will achieve. The use of a clicker can help, but, of course, it is better to adopt a style that minimises the risks. From the start, the archer should teach himself to draw with the sight already on the Gold and should do his best to avoid tension in the neck muscles.

Another frequent cause of tension is holding the aim too long. The eyes and the neck will tire, which causes wavering, and that prolongs the aiming period again, causing tension and so on. It is a vicious circle. Although some archers can hold and like holding their aim as long as 8sec, 2 to 4sec is enough for good shooting.

A last word on aiming: archers with good eyesight sometimes think the Gold is too large, too vague a mark to aim at. They choose a spot where the red and Gold meet and adjust their bowsight accordingly.

Lengthening your Range

As soon as you are doing well at 20yd, you will be eager to shoot further. Hitting a distant target is an exhilarating experience; indeed the first successful whack of an arrow at 100yd is almost difficult to believe. However, although there is no harm in 'having a go' at the long distances before you are ready for them, it would be unwise to monopolise precious space on the shooting line and go on shooting with experienced archers when you cannot yet group properly at 40yd. A good plan is to keep to a given range until you can 'group' regularly within the blue. Then increase your range by another 10yd and stick to the new distance until you can again put every arrow within the blue. Proceed steadily but surely; it will build up your confidence and fellow archers will applaud your commonsense.

Incidentally, there is no need to pull harder at the loose just because you are shooting further; your arrow will get there without extra help from you. Simply remember to bring down your sight and not to raise your bow arm. The change of elevation is done by moving the whole top half of your body, as one unit, from the waist.

Field style

Weather

'A little wynde in a moystie daye stoppeth the shafte more than a good wiskynge wynde in clere daye.' Like Roger Ascham, you will have to take note on the effects of weather. If, for instance, on a hot and humid summer's day, you find you cannot reach the target with your bowsight on the usual sight mark, do not start worrying about your technique but bring your sight down; it's the weather. Even without wynde, moystie dayes can reduce cast drastically.

The effects of wind, of course, are as varied as its varied aspects. Following or head winds offer no particular problems apart from a change of elevation. A following wind, naturally, makes your arrows overshoot the mark, and a head wind makes them drop short. A steady side wind can be countered by aiming off, but gusts can be rather testing. Aiming off then becomes pointless, as the wind can drop just as you have released. It is best to shoot on regardless, with the reassurance that other archers will do equally badly. Do not try to resist the violent squalls that push your arm off the mark; bring your bow down and wait for a momentary calm.

A lesser but more perfidious troublemaker is the isolated breeze that can blow at one end of the field and not at the other. Such breezes can occur when natural draughts or eddies are caused by houses, walls, trees or hillocks in the vicinity. It is quite possible to have a breeze blowing on the shooting line while the targets rest in perfect stillness; or vice versa. Passing clouds on a fine day will also cause disturbances worth watching for.

What Champions Are Made Of

Although the average archer can derive endless pleasure and interest from taking part in club shoots and regional tournaments, the next step on the ladder of competitive archery (national or international) will require a machine-like consistency in technique.

One of the reasons why rifle marksmen often find archery an exciting challenge is because of the delicate interplay of 'constants', of which archery has a greater number than in any other shooting sport. The Grand Master Bowman will have achieved a personal rhythm of shooting in which the following points seldom vary: draw-length – string alignment and anchor point – loose – straightness of bow arm – balance.

But to keep an unbroken rhythm throughout a tournament, say 288 arrows for a Double York Round, requires far more than fitness and good technique. It demands a power of concentration and self-discipline which can banish all emotions within and ignore disturbances without. The determined but placid man with a simple life stands a better chance of reaching the top, but the emotional archer with family problems, financial worries, or both, will win a double victory if he can forget about them, relax, and shoot a good score.

Now, though you may have read and digested all this and perhaps more, you will still make mistakes. The following checks should help you to trace them:

Arrows Widely Scattered all over the Target
Your bow is too strong for you and you can't hold your aim.

Arrows High

Anchor point too low – nocking point too low – leaning back – uneven pressure on drawing fingers – drawing more than usual – lower bracing height – dropped jaw – low elbow – nose not on the string – healing bow.

Arrows Right

Top limb tilted left – swinging bow arm – window too open – twisting bow on release by gripping too hard.

Arrows Left

Arm too stiff, string hitting bracer – string on right of chin – swinging bow arm – grip too tight – window too closed – top of bow tilted right – low bracing height – throwing drawing hand away on release – grabbing – sticky tab – plucking string.

Arrows Low

'Creeping' (your drawing hand moves forward on the loose) – bow arm sagging – bow hand dropping on release – anchor point too high – nocking point too high – overbraced bow.

Arrows Low Left

Gripping and arm much too stiff. Mistakes can also result from careless checking of equipment. With composite bows it is important to keep the bracing height as recommended by the makers. Beside affecting cast and accuracy, incorrect bracing height can have unpleasant effects: too low, and the bow may twang unnervingly and the string may even slap your arm above the bracer; too high and there may be undue strain, a kick on release, and even damage to the bow. (Bracing height can be altered by twisting or untwisting the string.) Another possible source of trouble is the bowsight. If the track is not fixed properly on the bow it will rattle on release and spoil concentration. Some bowsights can also slip down their tracks unnoticed, causing spectacular overshooting; which, of course, could be catastrophic indoors.

A bent arrow, even slightly so, is naturally useless. If an arrow glances off the boss, check it immediately; if it glances off the target stand, don't bother, it *is* bent!

Personal First-aid in Technique!

When your shooting has deteriorated and when friends or coaches have failed to bring lasting improvement, you will know that you are struggling against some hidden psychological barrier which has to be found and destroyed. It is either causing one specific mistake or, more likely, ruining your concentration and causing a whole range of different faults.

What is needed now is quiet practice *by yourself*, where the first exercise, beside deep breathing, will be the emptying of your mind of all negative emotions connected with archery or anything else. Shoot alone with peace within and without. *Don't score.* Just practise taking your time. THINK and FEEL until you have located a variance or an uncomfortable spot. Slow down your rate of shooting. Suddenly you might find, for instance, that your whole rhythm is improved beyond recognition by moving your drawing elbow a little up or a little down. Or you might become aware of some nervous tension which, although unconnected with archery, prevents you from holding your aim. Big or small, problems can be solved by a thorough but *unconcerned* study of yourself.

Here is a tip I stole from an American archer: he keeps a check-list with him and consults it if necessary. When you have done your self-analysis, you too could draw out a list of the faults which might crop up again under strain. I keep mine in my tackle box and, when I can remember to look at it, find it a great help. I will show it as an example of a personal check-list, but, of course, such lists are tailor-made and could not fit another archer.

- BREATHE.
- Relax jaw and shoulders.
- Don't poke, straighten up from head.
- Breathe.
- Draw FULLY.
- Lock back muscles.
- Don't DIG that string into your chin!
- Draw-hand towards neck, not outwards.
- Follow through.
- Breathe.
- Rest your eyes between each arrow.
- Don't talk between pairs.

Finally, a looking-glass piece of advice expressed some 2,500 years ago by Confucius: 'If, at any time, the feet of the Superior Man should slip, he acts like the archer who, when he misses the centre of the target, turns round and seeks the cause of failure in himself.'

Later, when you have acquired your personal rhythm and no longer have to think about technique, you may want to experiment with changes of style or equipment. Your precious, now unconscious, style will be disturbed for a while, and you will need the courage to persevere until you can see whether the change is effective or not.

Other Techniques

Power Archery

This originated in America. Whether it is a good or a bad technique is difficult to ascertain. Many British archers use the method and will go as far as to say that international championship standard cannot be achieved without it, but most GNAS coaches disapprove of it. For them, and for exponents of the conventional English style, it would appear, at first sight, that power archery is a very efficient method for making lame ducks walk straight. Its elimination of variables by sheer use of force and with the added support of more technical aids (extended bowsights, string peep holes, etc) achieves results which, we say, can equally well be achieved by improving one's own standard technique. I personally feel that this method, together with the use of poker stabilisers, does much to rob archery of its intrinsic

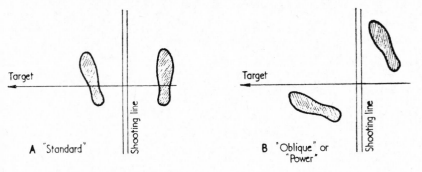

Fig 8. The stance – standard and oblique

beauty and dignity, and will gladly dispense with the extra points they might bring me in tournaments.

However, to twist a proverb 'one man's poison is another man's meat', power archery should by no means be rejected outright. When you feel confident enough, you may want to experiment with it, and find that it suits you. Briefly, the main difference from the English standard technique is that everything that can be locked is locked: knees are locked, the left shoulder is hunched forward and the bow arm held as rigid as a tree trunk. This allows the use of maximum force and steadiness but requires a different stance (fig 8) in which the body almost faces the target. Whatever your own style, you will find much of interest in Dave Keaggy's book on power archery, a very thorough and serious work.

Instinctive or Field Technique

Bow hunters cannot ask their victims to stand still while they pace the distance to set their sights. The last war's commandos who used archery to kill silently, contemporary archers who shoot small game in Britain and big game abroad, and the roving, golf and field archers, all have one thing in common: they can immediately ascertain the range and instinctively know the correct point of aim (the latter usually being short of the mark – see fig 9).

Choosing the point of aim for natural or instinctive shooting is done entirely by feel and can only be acquired with practice. Apart from the aiming method, the style also differs. First, the arrow must be nearer the line of sight, so the anchor point will have to be nearer

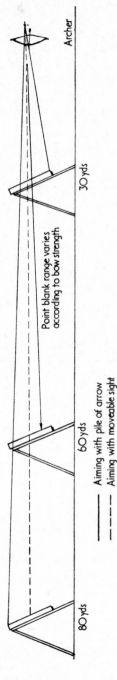

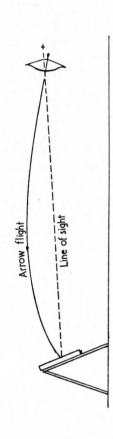

80 yds

60 yds

30 yds

Archer

Point blank range varies
according to bow strength

—— Aiming with pile of arrow
---- Aiming with moveable sight

N.B: The necessary elevation is achieved by moving the top half of the body from the waist, and will vary
according to the power of the bow

Arrow flight

Line of sight

Fig 9. Aiming – elevation

the eye. Some archers will use the corner of the mouth, others the cheekbone, the jaw, a tooth or any point in the face to which they can return for each shot. The bow and the head are canted right to give a better view of the mark, and the correct tilt of the bow has to be found with practice.

Learning to shoot the natural way can be done by shooting at a cardboard box in a large (and *grazed!*) field from varying distances (preferably not with your best set of championship arrows). Eventually you should be able to hit a wand at 20 or 25yd. Indeed, it is a most refreshing experience to leave your bowsight at home and go for a spot of roving with a friend.

If you wish to use the natural style in some form of competitive archery, you will have to join a field archery club and shoot in the 'bare-bow' class.

Perhaps you are now beginning to wonder why, if one can achieve such a degree of accuracy without any gadgets on the bow, the target archer should lumber himself with modern aids. There are two simple answers to this. A good instinctive shot demands a co-ordination of mind, eye and body near perfection. To repeat such a feat 144 or 288 times in the day would be impossible. Hunters will do more stalking than shooting and field archers only shoot four arrows in an end, with periods of waiting and walking between each target. Secondly, while the aiming 'gap' between the pile of the arrow and the mark is fairly easy to maintain constant below the target, this is far more difficult when above the target for the long distances.

5 The Club

The numerous advantages of belonging to a club have been touched on lightly earlier in this book; the time has come to review the subject more thoroughly. Without clubs, archery would be virtually non-existent; without a club, your own archery would not last more than a few months.

As I have already said, the lone beginner will probably not be able to afford the expense of a full-size target, will not benefit from friendly instruction, and will find that suitable fields are not available to single individuals. But what he will miss most of all is the camaraderie of fellow archers and the exciting awareness of taking part in today's exciting revival of archery. At the time of printing, Britain has over 670 clubs, with new ones springing up every season. France is next with 355 clubs, while Russia numbers a modest 37, exactly 30 more than Eire.

Joining a Club

All established British clubs are affiliated to the Grand National Archery Society (GNAS), itself affiliated to the Fédération Internationale de Tir à L'Arc, better known as FITA. The best way to discover your nearest club, or clubs, is to write to the regional secretary. Addresses of current secretaries of archery societies can be found in the magazines *The British Archer* and *Archery World* (USA).

Choice of a club will first be governed by availability of transport. If you drive or have a friend with a car, you will obviously have more freedom of choice than if you depend on public transport. However, one car-less member I know shoots with the London archers during the week, with another club on Saturdays and another on Sundays; where there is a will. . . .

If you live in a well-populated, prosperous locality, where archery is at its liveliest, you could be in the lucky position of being able to pick and choose your club. It might not be irrelevant, therefore, to give some idea of the main types of club you might find.

Gentle Clubs

Often made up of a small group of friends who have been shooting regularly for as many as fifteen, twenty or more years, they preserve peace and strict routine by keeping change and young people at bay. They are not particularly anxious to take part in tournaments or to

Shooting analysis in uncertain weather; county coach helping the Friars Gate Archers

organise matches, and, though they are usually made up of kind and polite people, they have no burning desire to promote archery by encouraging beginners. They simply want to shoot, which they do in the summer only. Before I am accused of sounding critical, I hasten to add that members of such clubs are true lovers of archery and, when prompted, often reveal a deep knowledge of a sport they practised very actively in their youth. They are invariably gentlemen in the best sense of the word, and shooting with them can be delightfully refreshing. If you already have your own equipment, can shoot reasonably well and do not wish to be too active, this may be just the kind of club you want.

Happy-Go-Lucky Clubs

They are usually the product of keenness and poor organisation. A characteristic sight during one of their practices is a sort of rush-hour agitation. People shoot and retrieve arrows with complete disregard for their neighbours on other targets; children, too many of them, shoot together without supervision, more often than not with defective tackle; beginners are allowed to develop bad faults from the start; banter and sarcasm are heard on the shooting line; and at the other end of the field unsecured targets occasionally fall off their stand, probably in despair, breaking and bending a few sets of arrows in the process.

Such clubs rarely belong to the GNAS (or NAA), seldom take part in matches and never in tournaments. They survive because there are probably no other clubs in the vicinity. They may even boast a long list of members, but members come and go as quickly as arrows fly, while out of the half-dozen founder-members, five will bash on at their targets, blissfully oblivious of the puzzled, rowdy, frightened or abashed newcomers who came with hopes of learning the noble art of archery. As for the sixth founder-member – the poor chap with a conscience – he is rushing here and there like a butterfly on the verge of a breakdown. Now and then he pauses briefly to puff at a cigarette and glances at his expensive composite bow. With luck, he might have time to shoot a dozen arrows before the day is over.

Spectacular changes can occur, of course. Energetic and clear-headed men with tact can shake lethargic committees out of their complacency, while on the other hand the rot can set in for the most dynamic clubs. It is up to you really. One way or the other you can influence your club.

Dynamic Clubs

These clubs are determined to take a significant part in the great upsurge of the sport. They usually benefit from having a nucleus of serious but cheerful archers capable of teaching beginners as well as training a team for competitions. Such clubs are for ever on the go, always exploring new ideas, endlessly chatting about the last shoot, match or tournament, discussing techniques or how to help so-and-so, etc. They will attend regional AGMs, courses and lectures and read the latest works on archery. They run their shooting by GNAS or NAA rules, and, though they welcome newcomers, will exercise a certain amount of care in selection, with safety and manners in mind. Finally, as long as the ground is not under three feet of water or frozen solid, they will shoot on through the year.

There are, in fact, a good many clubs of this kind, and they are obviously ideal for beginners.

Etiquette

When you join a club, someone should first of all teach you the safety rules. Then, by and by, you should be initiated gently into the archer's code of behaviour or etiquette. Most of it is simple commonsense, meant to make archery enjoyable and to preserve good humour while not spoiling other people's concentration. Etiquette helps a club to run smoothly and is a must in tournaments.

General. Do not talk in a loud voice when others are shooting.

Do not talk to an archer who obviously prefers to be left alone.

Do not offer advice unless asked for.

Do not exclaim on the shooting line (either in joy or disgust. Swear words should be expressed inwardly, but your whole archery will benefit if bad temper can be banished altogether).

Do not touch other archers' equipment without their permission.

Do not linger while retrieving arrows or walking back from the target.

Do not leave litter.

Do leave that transistor at home!

Do keep young children and dogs well back from the shooting line and, if possible, out of earshot.

Do not inflict your problems on other archers when shooting is going on; they have their own.

Do not go on using club equipment too long; other newcomers will need it.

Do not laugh when a good archer is going through a bad patch; it's a desperate business, and you won't escape it.

Target Days, Matches, Tournaments. Do not be late. Besides causing confusion, you will have to forfeit the number of arrows you haven't shot, or may not be allowed to shoot at all.

Leave nothing on the shooting line, except for foot markers (but don't leave them behind when changing distances or going home).

When shooting in twos do not place yourself on the centre mark.

Keep your equipment behind the waiting line.

Do not walk up and down the line comparing scores.

Give your score to the target captain in the following way: highest numbers first, and in two groups of three, eg 7–5–5– pause 3–1–1. Thank him at the end of the Round. (Taking down and adding up scores isn't everybody's idea of fun. The trend nowadays is to share the work if the appointed captain agrees.)

Retrieve arrows which have dropped *in front of the target* before the scores are taken down.

Do not pass *behind the target* before the scores have been recorded.

Keep to the left when leaving the shooting line or walking beyond the target.

Pay on the spot if you damage somebody's arrows through carelessness.

If you have shot badly, do not spoil your friends' success with your misery.

Teaching such a code of elementary courtesy would appear to be a little presumptuous – it all seems so obvious! But it is easy for the nervous beginner or even for the over-anxious budding champion to *forget* it!

Forming a New Club

The first obvious reason for starting an archery society of your own is that there is not one within reasonable reach. Or perhaps you feel that such a challenge has an irresistible appeal, or that the club you have been shooting with is not quite as congenial as you had hoped. Finally, you may already have a group of archer friends and you simply wish to shoot together on regular days. This would be the start of a 'Gentle' or of a 'Closed' Club. The former must be financed from the outset; the latter, usually being within a firm, a factory or a branch of the forces, usually enjoys financial backing. Whatever kind of club you have in mind, the following notes should provide some useful suggestions.

Starting from Scratch (first year)

It is quite feasible to start a club with only two archers, one at least being fairly experienced and the other a staunch friend, keen of eye and sound of body. For some time, they will not need to bother about committees and constitutions, and their main objective will be to become good enough to inspire confidence; this means hitting the target at 60yd and grouping well at the shorter distances. The problems of finding a suitable field will be dealt with in detail presently; at this stage, our two founder-members may have to be content with butts which will eventually become unsuitable. Short grass, storage for targets and level ground are needed, of course, but at this stage the field does not have to be more than 80yd long and can still be fairly narrow. Friendly farmers and headmasters are the most likely people to help you. You can buy a target if you can afford it or bales will do, with cardboard to stick the face on, not forgetting that target archery requires the centre of the Gold – or pin hole – to be 130cm above the ground.

During the gestation period, while you are acquiring and consolidating technique, you should read as much as you can about archery and try to attend one or two archery courses (write to the Sports Council, the Secretary of the GNAS or to the Central Council of Physical Recreation, or to the NAA of the United States). The following are recommended for club organisers: *The British Archer* magazine, published six times a year; the *Bowman's Handbook*, a mine of useful and interesting information; the GNAS *Rules of Shooting*, the International Archery Association (FITA) *Official Shooting Rules*, and the NAA *Official Tournament Rules*. All are available from archery dealers, of whom the best in Britain is undoubtedly D.G. Quick of Portsmouth.

May is the best time to start, and by July or August the club should begin to shape up.

First Members

When you are confident that you can teach beginners safely and in line with standard technique, the time has come to find members. In a fairly well populated area you may run the risk of getting more members than you can handle. So start in a modest way, simply talking to people you know; you will be surprised to find how many apparently unlikely individuals are keen to have a go. Now, what about equipment? Newcomers wanting to find out what archery is like cannot be expected to come already equipped, hence the need for club tackle. The minimum to start with is two practice fibreglass bows (one at 26lb and one at 28lb), one set of eight 28in metal arrows (making it two sets of four, one set distinguished from the other by extra cresting – paint or tape), two bracers, two tabs and two ground quivers. When the club starts making money, there is no reason why you should not reimburse yourselves for these expenses. With two of you teaching not more than four candidates, one target is all you want. But now is not too soon to start taking good care of your bosses.

No matter how tempting it is, do not overload your beginners with technical information; all they want is to shoot and, preferably, hit the target. The latter should be placed at 15 or 20yd, near enough and far enough to ensure a feeling of achievement in your pupils. Even at the first attempt, they must feel that they have learnt something worth learning. This will mean care, friendliness and perhaps firmness on your part.

Targets

These are the most expensive and valuable items in club equipment. Although the object of archery is to fill them full of holes, one naturally wants to put off their eventual demise as long as possible. The two parts most exposed to ill-treatment are the outside rim and the centre. Two people carrying a target will pull it out of shape, and so will rolling it and propping it against a wall. Target bosses should be stored flat on the floor or stacked in vertical *racks*. As soon as the centre becomes soft, you can insert a piece of hardboard between the target and the stand. Besides prolonging the life of bosses, good care will avoid waves and hollows – a common reason for 'bouncers'.

Trolleys can be made or bought for carrying targets, but by far the easiest method is to carry them on your back. Taking the target from the stand (don't forget to unfasten it!), put your hands behind your back level with your hips, grab hold of the target and unbalance it until it rests flat on your back, then keep your back straight and don't lean too far forward – you will be surprised to see how easy it is to walk, even to run with a target 'in your hands'! Picking up a target from the ground needs strong leg and stomach muscles, so you should start with one knee down and then rise.

Besides 'how to shoot', first-day archers should be taught how to withdraw arrows from the target and from the ground so as not to bend them. They should be told to pull in line with the shaft, with the pulling hand near the pile. When withdrawing from the target, the other hand should be pressed firmly against the target face.

Withdrawing arrows from the target

Carrying the target: no effort if done the right way

As with all pupils, you will have the occasional paragons who listen, take in and do what they are told. They present no problem, except that they might soon outshine you! They are the nucleus of a future team and care must be taken that they do not lose their confidence by attempting too much too quickly. At the other end of the scale many beginners are somewhat perplexed to find that shooting with a bow and arrows is far more difficult than they thought. Some may react by using brute force and shooting fast without taking in advice; and others may be overawed and need encouragement − these may even have to start at 10yd only. Practically anybody can become good enough at archery to enjoy it provided he has one essential quality: determination.

So, your beginners have come back. You should now let them practise by themselves more and more, while making sure that the safety checks become second nature to them and that they do not lapse into some serious mistakes. A constant anchor point is the chief point to insist on.

Now is also a good time to make new members share in non-shooting activities like putting targets away, cutting grass, cleaning arrows, etc. Some of the important work is going to take place with a tankard of beer in your hand or round a cup of tea or coffee. If the newcomers are sufficiently fired with the idea of a new club, the time has come for planning and organising.

Shooting Field

You may have had to improvise until now, but, with a growing club, suitable amenities are essential. In addition to the already mentioned low grass and storage place for bosses, you must be able to accommodate four or five targets. With 8ft between them and 10yd clearance on either side, the shooting area must be at least 25 yd wide. The same distance is also recommended behind the targets, plus 10yd behind the shooting line (see fig 10), which gives us 135yd minimum length, allowing for a shooting distance of 100yd. And of course the unmentionable must be mentioned: since no one can shoot straight unless nature's call can be satisfied, a 'convenience' should be available.

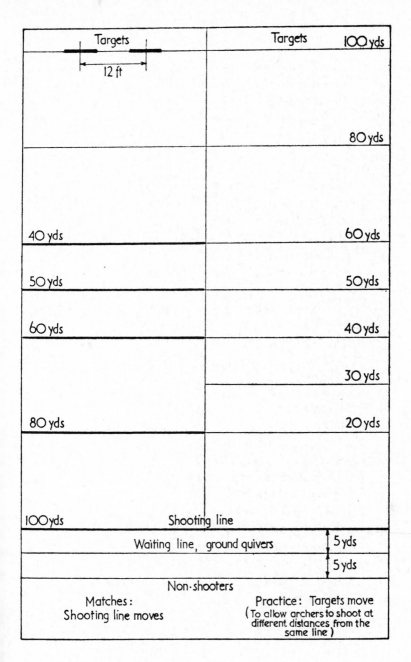

Fig 10. Layout of archery field

The ideal field would be the one you could buy or rent purely for your own use. But, difficult to find; beside luck, you would need more money than is usually available, both for the cost of the field and for the cost of suitable mowing machines. Putting aside exceptionally fortunate circumstances, we are left with four possibilities: 'stately homes and lesser manors', private schools, state schools and local recreation grounds. Whatever authorities you approach, it is wise not to appear too casual, either in dress or manners. The first impression is vital: archers are quiet, pleasant, sensible people who practise a serious sport and do *not* 'play' with bows and arrows. They have strict safety rules *and* a third-party insurance.

If you have one of the 'stately homes and lesser manors' in the neighbourhood, you will lose nothing by asking. Archery blends well with English parkland and history, and it also attracts visitors. If you wear archery colours and are polite to His Lordship, he may well let you shoot on one of his lawns.

Private schools often welcome archers with open arms, especially if you offer to teach archery to the pupils. The advantages are numerous; the grounds are usually well kept throughout the year, the schools charge nominal or no fees, there are no forms or red-tape, you may come as you please in the holidays and there is very probably an existing shelter to store targets. The most obvious drawback would be no shooting on Saturday afternoons in term-time. Find a list of boys' and girls' schools in your area, and write rather than telephone, stating your aim briefly but carefully and asking when you could come to talk it over. They may want to be reassured about safety and whether you would respect their grounds (often a beautiful and congenial setting). On your part, you will want your club evenings, afternoons or mornings to be interfered with as little as possible.

State Schools and Recreation Grounds are often the only islands of green grass where cement and concrete dominate the scenery. As a rule, obtaining permission to shoot will be delayed by official red-tape; and, if successful, you must remember that permission is generally only given for a year, and you must not forget to renew your application. The lower ranks of officialdom, while harbouring genuine friends of archery, also have their fair share of distrustful ignorance. One club, applying for permission to shoot on some council grounds, was told that its members could do so, *provided that their arrows were fitted with rubber blunts!*

You will be confronted with many lesser problems once you have cut through the red-tape. You may have approached a headmaster successfully (the final yes comes from the educational authority, but he can still say NO), and have received the right number of forms to fill in, in duplicate or in triplicate, but you may still find that the caretaker refuses to lend his keys or to come out to open the school at weekends. So, perhaps a chat with the latter might be the first thing to do. Also, you may find the problem of safety on recreation grounds acute, for some we know are shared by as many as seventeen sports clubs.

Whatever the type of location, you must have facilities to store targets or permission to put up a hut.

How to Lose Your Field

You can easily lose your field if you drive on wet or frosty turf, frighten the public, are noisy, leave litter, or forget that the staff, children and parents of a school have priority, even if they will choose to walk behind the targets while you are shooting.

Finances

When starting on such a small scale, the founder members will have to finance the initial outlay, and may not feel inclined to pay a subscription on top of that. However, the habit of putting something in the kitty every time you shoot (green fee or shooting fee) is essential if the club is to survive.

Still Growing (second and third year)

When the membership has grown from four to, say, eight the organisation of the club must become more formal. A provisional subscription fee must be agreed upon (this varies from one to five pounds, with special rates for juniors); an entry fee at this stage may hamper the growth of the club. For the sake of simplicity, it may be a good idea to include the various affiliation and insurance charges in the subscription. Legal covering is included in the GNAS affiliation.

A skeleton committee can now be formed, including at least a secretary, a treasurer, and a coaching officer whose job is to see that coaching duties are fairly shared by and with all those concerned. They will have to decide how soon they can afford to buy what club equipment is required, who from and how much. Too little equipment will cause waiting, and too much can make new members think that they do not really have to buy their own. In our experience, four sets of tackle is about right (1 for women/juniors, 2 for average man, 1 for extra strong or tall man). A second target will become necessary.

Prospective new members will contact you because they have heard of your club through your own public relations activities or simply hearsay. A good club must grow fairly slowly to avoid chaos. Although, in principle, you will welcome anyone interested in archery, a certain selectivity must be applied; not socially, of course – archery is one of the most mixed and democratic sports on earth – but with an eye on the happy and safe running of the club. It should be shown by your own behaviour that quietness, good temper and friendliness make up the visa for your society. Safety rules should be typed and shown to all newcomers, and persistent breaking of these result in dismissal.

The proportion of juniors to seniors in a club is a delicate subject. No club worth its salt would not be proud to train a junior team or simply to encourage future archers. But young people, when not awed by a massive majority of elders, *will* herd together and start skylarking noisily. It is a good idea to insist on a parent being present with children under 12, and older juniors should show their desire to become good archers and prove that they are not just 'kids wanting to play Robin Hood games'. A happy proportion of juniors should be about one-fifth of the total membership.

Archery itself selects its true followers, but before the unsuitable members have discovered that archery is not their sport they can do a fair amount of damage. Make all newcomers pay their shooting fee from the second week, and wait at least for a further three weeks before you ask for their subscription; you might have to return it.

Organising the Shooting
Practice without scoring is all right when you start shooting at a new distance, but you will soon want to see how you are improving. If

you are taking down scores for each dozen, and you shoot six, eight or nine dozens, you might as well shoot one of the official Rounds (see p 96). Besides preparing the club for matches and tournaments, shooting the Rounds creates the necessary stimulation. If your club meets twice a week, you could have an ordinary practice in the evening and shoot a Round on your morning or afternoon shoot. The long Rounds (12 dozen) take all day but the others (9, 8 and 6 dozens) can be shot inside two hours. Two of the favourite rounds for new clubs are the Windsor and the Short Metric.

At regular intervals clubs organise what are known as Target Days – a meeting when a Round is shot formally, under tournament conditions. Members wear their greens and shoot three arrows alternately, starting each end and moving from the shooting line at the field captain's whistle. The scores, taken by the target captains (usually no. 3 on target list), are collected by the records officer and entered in the record book. Medals are given to the mens', ladies' and juniors' champions. It is up to the Committee to decide on the frequency of target days. Once a month, twice a year, it will depend on the general feeling and other activities.

Coaching versus Team

Two distinct and important activities will now be taking place side by side: instructing the beginners and preparing a Team for matches and tournaments. Unless this preparation is planned carefully, there is the danger that the best archers will lose precious practice time by doing too much instructing. They may, in self-defence, give up coaching altogether and this will result in 'sloppy' club archery. The only way out of this dilemma is a duty roster shared by the more experienced archers, so that those who are off duty can practise with a clear conscience. One could, perhaps, have two duty instructors once a week, sharing the morning between them. If the field is large enough, the team or future team could shoot well away from the beginners, in Olympic remoteness. An extra evening's practice by themselves would, of course be most beneficial.

Instruction for Beginners

This should follow the recommended sequence: 1. Description of tackle and archery vocabulary. 2. Safety rules and care of tackle. 3.

Checking dominant eye. 4. Finding arrow length. 5. Position of pin. 6. Position on the line. 7. Holding the bow. 8. Turning the head. 9. Nocking arrow. 10. Fingers on string, prep line. 11. Loosing in the ground. 12. Position on line again plus drawing. 13. Aiming and drawing, holding, loosing. 14. Follow-through. 15. Walk to target and withdraw arrows. 16. Adjust pin.

'And he that wyl not knowe his faulte shall never amende it.' After a few months, a new archer will need what we call 'Shooting analysis'. Minor faults may have developed, which prevent his shooting from being quite as good as it could be. This analysis is a delicate piece of guidance and will sort out the good from the not so good coaches. The most precious unconscious skill an archer can acquire is 'personal rhythm'; this, once lost or disturbed, can take weeks or months to recover. It is only too easy to ruin a potential champion with the wrong advice!

The coach helping to trace a hidden fault or faults should not stand too close, and should keep watching for several ends without saying anything, even if he thinks he has spotted the trouble. He will first look for the obvious faults: varying draw-length (sagging arm or inconsistent back tension) – forward or creeping loose – snatching – inconsistent or bad anchor – string allowed to ease away before release – tight grip – stiff bow arm – hunched shoulder – no follow-through – snap shooting.

Look for faults by moving to the three (safe) sides of the archer. Watch for tension in hands and neck muscles. When you have seen something apparently wrong, think before you speak. The observed archer will not shoot badly all the time, but he may unconsciously correct his faults when being watched; give him time to relax into his best or his worst style. Now watch how the arrows fly. If they fly straight in spite of a departure from orthodox technique, leave bad alone and look again for real trouble. When no faults at all can be traced, the cause could be something as simple as a bad tab, too high a sight mark, or unsuitable arrows. In short, don't rush in with advice and *never* believe what helped you will automatically help another.

Excellent coaching courses are run by the GNAS and CCPR but the little help given in this book should fill a few gaps before you can attend one of them.

When courage and friendliness meet: instructing

Matches

The chief pleasure derived from matches is meeting other archers. Either as hosts to or guests of friendly clubs, you will experience the tangible proof that you are not alone in the pursuit of an apparently obscure sport. Looking at random through the Southern Counties

Wheelchair archer with home-made stabilisers

Archery Society's *Annual Report*, I can count over fifty clubs in Sussex and Surrey alone; county and local clubs proliferate in the USA.

The best way to arrange the first matches is to ask your regional secretaries for a list of societies and to write to the nearest one, inviting them for a short Round. You should state the number of archers you can accommodate (never more than six per target, shooting in two lots of threes) and give clear instructions on how to reach you. On the day, you should come early to set out the field properly with shooting line, waiting line and distances clearly marked, and your targets numbered, with a corresponding number on the shooting line. Use proper score sheets (from archery dealers) clipped on hardboard, marked with the target number and equipped with sharp pencils. If you can put small flags at the various distances or on the targets, it will provide a useful guide for possible wind. Have all this ready before the visitors come, and don't forget to organise the wives for refreshments.

For the actual shooting, a field captain must be appointed, shooting or non-shooting. The scoring is shared between the two clubs. Should one team have more archers than the other, the number of scores taken will be that of the smaller side against the same number of the top scores of the other.

Before launching out into matches, it is advisable to wait until you have at least six archers capable of shooting reasonably well at 80yd. It is not usual nor desirable to use the handicap system for inter-club matches.

It might not be amiss to advise the younger members not to appear too jubilant if their team wins, or too disgruntled if they lose. What matters is a good day's shooting with convivial friends.

Established Clubs

After three years, the new club will start sliding downhill, or will grow from strength to strength. Nothing that lives can remain stationary for very long. When sheer physical growth becomes unadvisable, variety and change must be brought in.

Displays

With the expanding popularity of archery, clubs are often asked to give *displays* at country shows and fêtes. They need not be considered as a somewhat debasing kind of circus act, for they serve a threefold purpose: they are usually for some charity, they can rectify the public's views on archery and they can bring clubs new members. But only competent and well-established clubs should tackle such a venture. The main idea of these displays is to make money, and no one is going to pay to watch a few archers shoot at a target: the public will want to, and should be encouraged to, 'have a go' themselves; this is where the words danger, chaos and fiasco can loom large unless the whole operation is run on near-military lines.

First, the safety requirements should be made absolutely clear on *paper* to the organisers and, before the display, you should go and check that they have been adhered to. Should the arrangements look unsuitable or unsafe, have no hesitation in walking out – there is too much at stake.

The shooting area should be roped in and set out as in the sketch (fig. 11).

The actual display is best kept short and may be repeated two or three times during the day, lasting no more than fifteen minutes each time. You will, of course, use your best archers, and perform the various kinds of 'variety shoots' which appeal to the public. As a rule, they will not appreciate your accuracy unless it is linked with some spectacular feats. Popping balloons at 25 yd will raise more enthusiasm than hitting the gold at 100 yd. Use your imagination to devise games between two archers or between two teams which the spectators can clearly follow, and make sure that they work. If clearly marked on white paper, noughts and crosses can be quite exciting; so can horizontal Popinjay shot at with blunt heads, and shooting an apple off a dummy's head; but, in the end, anything with balloons remains the great favourite.

If the day is successful, your displays will be but brief moments of relaxation between long periods of hard work. On a fine July afternoon, you may well be shepherding crowds of would-be archers from 2 to 7 pm! After appearing in half a dozen such shows, our club adopted a routine which aims to achieve speed, smoothness and safety, as follows.

The shooting area has one entrance and one exit clearly marked. People queue *outside* the area and are only allowed in as places become vacant. One club member sits at the entrance collecting money and pointing out the available instructor. We have two archers per target, with ground quivers, fibreglass bows and six arrows per person, which they shoot in threes or sixes according to what they pay. Only club archers are allowed beyond the shooting line to retrieve arrows. Instruction is kept simple, giving the public the best chance of hitting the target, guiding their arm if necessary. Composite bows are never lent, as this could mean dangerous overshooting. Answering questions about archery or about our club is the job of one club member, who just acts as information officer.

The shooting public varies tremendously – from plump ladies who refuse to take off their coats to nervous children who say 'yes, yes' and do everything wrong, from apparent louts to real clergymen and army crack-shots puzzled at missing that big target – and includes of course, the gifted individual who has, now and again, to be shooed away gently to make room for others. As a rule, respect for archery is born the moment you place bows and arrows in their hands.

If the fair is held in your area, you are almost bound to make the odd new member or two (keep a notebook handy for names and addresses). Some of our best archers and friends were found this way.

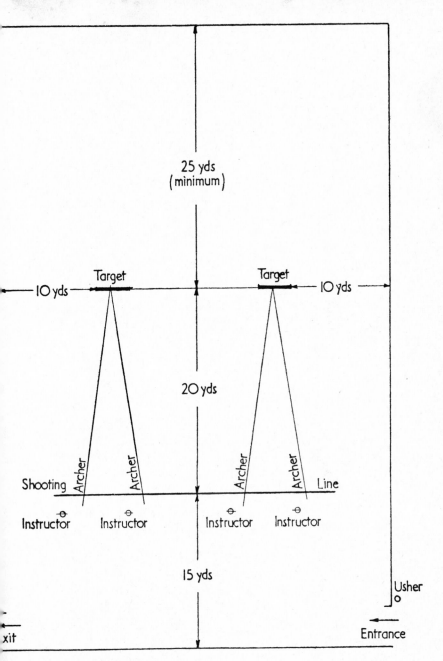

Fig 11. Layout of field for displays

The financial side of displays will vary according to the views of the club and show committees. The wear and tear on targets and arrows will be pretty heavy, and there will be the cost of transporting bosses. Splitting the proceeds fifty-fifty usually seems agreeable to all. $2\frac{1}{2}$p for three arrows and 5 p for six is cheap enough to attract the public and can make up to £6 by the end of a good day. It is wise to refuse to hand over the money to collectors, with or without official badges, but to take the final bag to the treasurer when all is over.

Club Business

After two or three years the club will have gained enough members and experience to make the final adjustments in organisation. What will vary from club to club is the degree of formality with which the meetings are conducted.

In addition to safety rules there is obviously a need for a minimum list of 'constants' in club activities, such as one weekly practice meeting from May to October, one monthly handicap meeting, two target days in the year, two or three matches and two general meetings to discuss and plan the society's business; with dates to be typed and handed out to members at least two weeks ahead. As far as the main events can be foreseen, a provisional fixture list should be drafted in the winter and sent to all members in April. All other activities should be arranged as far ahead as possible, and club members will rise to impromptu challenges without printed rules telling them to do so.

When the membership has reached its ceiling, the committee could be re-elected, with the addition of further officers as required. The secretary, who usually knows more about the club than anybody else, should be encouraged to stay in office for two or three year periods. Other members (including a lady if possible) must be given the opportunity to stand down if they are tired or want to give a chance to someone else. It is important that non-committee members should be encouraged to take part in informal discussions concerning the club, to suggest ideas and to take on responsibilities. Never should founder-members think that the ways in which they first ran the club are still necessarily the best. In our case the agonising boredom of listening to minutes being rattled off in liturgic monotone has been dispensed with. We note down the main points of the meeting, these are typed and copies are sent to all members. The history of the club is preserved by means of a twice-yearly *Newsletter*. It is fun to read through the pages of old *Newsletters*, to recall nearly forgotten incidents and to see, sometimes with amazement, how quickly the club has grown.

A dynamic club will have to decide, perhaps reluctantly, to limit its membership. This is the best way to avoid congestion on the shooting line and to preserve the all-important feeling of unity. But even with a fixed maximum, members will drop out and newcomers will join – a fluctuation at once both sad and desirable. A manageable number would seem to be about thirty, which is enough to ensure a regular attendance of 12 to 16 members and for the club to pay its way. With subscriptions of, say, £4 for seniors and half that for juniors, not counting insurance, you could average around £94 a year plus shooting fees (which could bring in some £12 a month) – quite enough to buy and maintain five targets, club equipment and prizes, pay the rent and print the *Newsletter*.

Clubs in Britain doing pretty well financially and wishing not to arouse the interest of tax inspectors should bear in mind that only income arising from investment or from trading outside the club is liable to be taxed. It is, therefore, simpler to spend what you have on improving amenities, and to reduce the shooting fee (always a popular move). It is almost impossible to have too big an income. What with the new indoor range, winter dance, instructors' courses, hiring films, club library, etc, a surplus will soon go. And remember, to be officially recognised, a club must have a constitution.

Archery in Schools

Archery is becoming increasingly popular in all kinds of schools. In addition to its universal appeal and beneficial effects . . . its educational value should also be stressed. Besides developing co-ordination, self-control and determination, it can offer a tremendous uplift to children who do not shine in team games. The confidence gained will not only make the pupil happier but will also influence his work favourably. The founder of Harrow School was well aware of this in the late sixteenth century when he included the following lines in the curriculum: 'You shall allow your child at all times, bows, shafts, bowstring and bracer to exercise shooting.'

Running a school club has a few problems, the first being the necessity for an archer among the staff. Visiting instructors are still hard to come by. Although keenness in the school instructor is enough to start things going, he generally has to improve himself quickly, for his experience is often limited to 'having a go' with wooden tackle. Many schoolmasters in charge of archery shoot in blissful ignorance of safety precautions and standard technique. They should visit the nearest archery club as soon as possible and talk with experienced archers. If their timetable allows them they should also shoot with the club and attend an instructors' course. Another 'must' is to join the Association for Archery in Schools (see appendix), from which they will derive useful advice as well as information for inter-school matches and tournaments. *The British Archer* magazine always has a few pages devoted to junior archery, with notes on coaching and information about competitions, and in the USA *Archery World* and *Bow and Arrow* include notes on family events.

As all schoolmasters know, children have a magical gift for being in more than one place at once, hence an even greater necessity for stringent safety rules. They also have a natural leaning towards dumping toys or tools on the ground to dash off to some new activity. This won't do with archery tackle. Stop five minutes before time and make sure they put the equipment away carefully.

6 Target Business

The rounds

In target archery you shoot six arrows and call it an END; but that is only the beginning! Counting the sighting end (sighters) you shoot twenty-five ends in a York, Hereford or FITA Round; of fifty ends in a Double York, Hereford or FITA Round.

A Round consists of a certain number of arrows shot at various distances to suit various classes of archers. The longest distances are 100yd and 90m for men and 80yd and 70m for ladies. Unlike the practice in rifle shooting, the longest range is shot first; you then move closer or the targets are brought forward. This custom dates from the days when the practice of archery was not just a pleasant pastime — unless the enemy fled at the first volley of arrows, the distance between the archers and their mark would gradually, perhaps swiftly, decrease.

The idea of shooting Rounds evolved in the latter half of the eighteenth century. In those days, targets were lined up at both ends of the field and archers shot three arrows each way. But in 1828 an American club cut the number of targets needed by half with the simple expedient of shooting ends of six arrows at a single line of butts. With their customary speed in adopting alien ideas, the British followed suit in 1949. Apart from this, the practice of target archery has remained much the same since 1787 when the Prince Regent took an active interest in toxophily, helping to establish the system of five scoring zones.

Modern Rounds can be divided into three groups: British, American and Continental. Even limiting our list to Rounds shot in Britain, there are still enough of them to suit all manner of archers and clubs. An up-to-date list of Rounds shot in Britain can be found in the GNAS Rules of Shooting.

The Rounds shot in major tournaments are the York, the Hereford and the FITA rounds shot twice over two days ('Double York', etc). More and more organisers are adopting the FITA round, which, in my opinion, is a little sad. One should not be branded as an incorrigible reactionary for preferring names like St George or York to something quite so lacking in glamour and imagination as FITA. Granted, the international teams, present and future, should practise the round chosen by the Fédération Internationale de Tir à l'Arc and the 50 and 30m shot on the 80cm face are certainly an interesting

Tournament: end of a 70m end. FITA Round

THE ROUNDS

SENIORS

1. Yards—(122cm 5-zone faces)

arrows	doz	yd	yd	yd	ends	app* time
144	6 / 4 / 2 / — / 12	100 / 80 / 60 — YORK	80 / 60 / 50 — HEREFORD		24	4hr
108	3 / 3 / 3 / — / 9	100 / 80 / 60 — ST GEORGES	80 / 60 / 50 — ALBION	60 / 50 / 40 — WINDSOR	18	3hr
96	4 / 4 / — / 8	100 / 80 — NEW WESTERN	80 / 60 — LONG WESTERN	60 / 50 — WESTERN	12	2hr
72	4 / 4 / — / 8	100 / 80 — NEW NATIONAL	80 / 60 — LONG NATIONAL	60 / 50 — NATIONAL	16	2hr 40min
60	5	20 — PORTSMOUTH (Indoor—10-zone 60cm face)			20	3hr 20min
90		AMERICAN — 30 arrows at 60yd / 30 arrows at 50yd / 30 arrows at 40yd			15	2½hr

2. *Metres (122cm 10-zone faces for 90 and 70m—80cm 10-zone faces for 50m and less)*

Metres

144	90 ⎫ 70 ⎬ FITA 50 ⎪ men 30 ⎭ 70 ⎫ 60 ⎬ FITA 50 ⎪ ladies 30 ⎭	36	6hr
72	50 ⎫ SHORT METRIC 30 ⎬	24	4hr
72	30 —— STAFFORD—(Indoor)	24	4hr
36	30 —— BRITISH ARCHER—(Outdoor)	12	2hr

Dozens: 3, 3, 3, 3 = 12 (FITA); 3, 3 = 6 (Short Metric); 6 (Stafford); 3 (British Archer).

*Club shooting time, not tournament. Including scoring but not chats at the target nor tea break.

CONVERSION TABLE

metres	yd	ft	in
1		3	3.37
5	5	1	4.85
30	32	2	5.10
50	54	2	0.50
60	65	1	10.20
70	76	1	7.90
90	98	1	3.30

challenge, but this is no reason why the traditional British rounds should be dropped, or their cheerfully neat five-zone target face. Even in their frantic anxiety to fall in line with the Continent, they still have a few native customs worth preserving.

Scoring

The five-zone standard British or NAA target is 4ft in diameter (122cm). The circle in the centre, or Gold, is 24.4cm in diameter and ringed by four concentric bands (red, blue, black and white), each measuring 12.2cm across. The scoring values are:

GOLD	9
RED	7
BLUE	5
BLACK	3
WHITE	1

The line marking the outermost edge of the white counts as within the scoring zone. An arrow touching two zones will score the higher one. The exact centre of the Gold is called the *pin hole*. In matches and tournaments it is customary to have a sweep for the arrow nearest to the pin hole in the last end of the day or the last end of the longest distance.

Arrows bouncing off the target ('bouncers') are usually not scored, but, provided there is time, one can go through the tedious process of ringing each arrow hole so that a bouncer will leave an unringed hole. But this is not always allowed, and, if you have two bouncers in the same end, you are left with a problem! However, a new rule allows witnessed bouncers to be shot again.

In matches and tournaments, archers usually shoot four per target in two details of two, shooting three arrows in turn. When everyone has shot his six arrows, the field captain blows his whistle and the field moves up to the targets to take down the scores of that end. The target captain (third on the target list) is responsible for writing down your score, which you call out clearly in two lots of three, starting with the highest. You are not allowed to touch or remove an arrow until all scores have been taken, and the target captain has the right to refuse to score an arrow touched by its owner, specially if the arrow is

Tournament: scoring

near the higher scoring zone. On paper faces in particular, pushing an arrow even slightly can widen the hole enough for an extra point.

The FITA, Metric, Portsmouth, and Stafford Rounds are shot on the Continental 10-zone face, where each of the five coloured zones are divided into two. Only the inner ring (the 10) counts as Gold; it is entered on the score sheets as an X. For the 50m, 30m and 20yd distances of the above rounds, shot on the 80cm face, only three arrows are shot in one end to minimise the risk of hitting nocks.

Archers should of course enter their scores in their own score books, which might be needed in case of doubt.

Classification Scheme and Handicap System

The classification scheme and the handicap system give archers clear goals to strive for. They are both used in tournaments to place archers into fairly even groups. An archer shooting to or over the required score three times in a calendar year can claim the title of 3rd, 2nd or 1st class archer. These three grades can be gained during any organised meeting shot under GNAS rules, but they are not registered or publicised by the GNAS.

The other two titles of Master Bowman and Grand Master Bowman call for much greater skill and consistency, and the latter can only be gained in major tournaments. Claims must be submitted to the GNAS Secretary who, on behalf of the National Council, will send the badge and publicise the award. On the same basis, other high rewards to be gained are the FITA badges.

Handicap System

Its twofold purpose gives a clear indication of the archer's standard and progress, and allows competitors of little experience to shoot alongside skilled veterans. As anyone who studies the handicap and allowance tables can see, the system is generous to beginners but ruthless to advanced archers who, in order to stay at the top, must constantly improve their scores.

Handicaps start at +60 and move down in even numbers to −40. To give an example of the two extremes, an archer shooting a York Round with a 60 handicap would be given an allowance of 600 points, while the −40 archer would have to score 400 points *before* he could start positive scoring.

Place		Date		
Round: Hereford		Hits	Score	Gold
5 5 5 3 3 —	5 3 3 1 1 —	10	34	—
5 5 3 1 1 —	7 7 5 1 — —	9	35	—
9 7 5 3 1 —	5 3 3 3 3 1	11	43	1
9 7 7 7 5 1	7 5 3 3 1 —	11	55	1
9 7 3 1 1 —	7 7 5 5 3 3	11	51	1
7 5 5 3 3 3	7 5 3 1 — —	10	42	—
Total at 80yd/m		62	260	3
9 9 7 7 7 5	9 7 5 5 3 1	12	74	3
9 9 7 7 3 1	9 7 7 5 5 5	12	74	3
9 7 7 5 3 1	7 7 5 5 5 3	12	64	1
9 5 5 5 1 —	7 7 7 3 1 1	11	51	1
Total at 60yd/m		47	263	8
9 7 5 5 5 3	9 9 5 5 3 3	12	68	3
9 9 7 7 5 5	9 9 7 7 5 5	12	84	4
Total at 50yd/m		24	152	7
H/cap 31 Class 3rd	Grand Total	133	675	18

Specimen entry in individual score book

The following examples will help to throw a little more light on the system, but, of course, the current handicap table, with its 1,064 handicap scores and 1,064 handicap allowances, *must* be bought!

THREE HANDICAPS FOR AN ALBION ROUND (1971)

Score	Handicap	Allowance	Total
277	60	474	751
740	2	11	751
941	−40	−190	751

Club records officers should enter each score made by each member together with the appropriate rating. An archer will be assessed for his first handicap when he has shot three complete rounds. From then on, his handicap will be reduced each time he shoots a better round. If an archer goes through a bad phase and goes on shooting below his better form, his handicap can be increased at his request by taking an average of all his rounds shot during the last calendar month, provided he has shot at least three rounds.

The handicap system has much to commend it, but suffers from a few intrinsic weaknesses – mainly, the difficulty of accurately assessing an archer's standard in the early stages, when his form can alternately reach unexpected heights as well as sink into gloomy quagmires, all within one season. A promising but inexperienced novice could be reluctant to shoot too many rounds on home grounds, as his current tournament allowances might become drastically reduced. There is also the sad fact that, if one or two competitors with childish minds and calculated casualness happen to give the wrong handicap at tournaments, they may go home with medals which rightly belong to somebody else.

SEASON .... NAME							
HANDICAP .... CLASS							
Date	Round	Meeting	Score	H/cap Rating	Class	Current Comp H/cap	Remarks

Example of Club Records Officers Book

Such record sheets can either be duplicated or bought.

Tournaments

Why Not?

There is no need to let your ego shrink too much at the mere mention of the word tournament. Any archer belonging to an affiliated club can take part. Obviously, it would be a little foolish to go when you still have difficulty in scoring at the long distances but, save for that proviso, a 3rd class archer can shoot in tournaments *and enjoy it.*

First you can choose the meeting to suit your skill. If you are not quite up to the 100yd or 90m ranges, you can attend a tournament where the Men's Hereford and Albion and the Ladies Windsor are shot (usually on handicap). You would indeed be an unusual person if you did not go to your first tournament with a stomachful of fluttering butterflies, but the general atmosphere of quiet sympathy and tact soon dispels your apprehension. I have a vivid memory of my first 'County Oak' in Brighton, where I shot my first arrow with a relaxed grip and no bowsling. My bow gleefully leapt out of my hand and landed a few feet ahead with resounding clatter. I was sure that the whole line of some 140 silent archers had heard and seen the shameful exhibition. My target neighbour simply winked at me and asked with a friendly smile: 'What are you shooting today? Your arrows or your bow?' As I shot the third arrow of that sighting end, my sight-track came unstuck practically all the way down, and sprang back and forth like a metronome. Without a word, another archer handed me a tube of adhesive. For my next tournament, my bow was secured to my wrist with a bowsling and my sight-track was screwed in!

Can you be too young or too old for an archery tournament? Well, young archers can consult the table of junior rounds to see what is expected of them, and for the 'old' ones there is practically no limit. In the 1950s one of the competitors in a major tournament was a lady of 90, and in the same decade an army major took up the sport at the age of 45 and became an international four years later. More recently, 47-year-old Flight Lieutenant Gray became Sussex champion less than a year after taking up archery. Physically handicapped archers can also shoot in tournaments and are allowed to have their arrows scored and retrieved by a friend. In fact, there is nothing uncommon in seeing wheelchair archers on the shooting line.

Where and When?

Remembering that you can only shoot in tournaments if you belong to a club affiliated to the GNAS or NAA, it follows that you will be issued with more or less up-to-date information. The trouble with *Newsletters* is that, though they might be bang up to date at the time of writing, when they eventually reach you they are no longer quite so topical. The only way to draw out a full list of British events for the year is to consult all the four sources available, namely the GNAS and regional *Newsletters*, *The British Archer* magazine and D. G. Quick's catalogue, with its 'dates to remember'. As an example of such a list of events, you could have seen that in 1970, three flight, six clout and

Junior championships – target business is serious business

eleven field shoots were held, as well as ninety-three target archery tournaments. The NAA's *Archery World* is also helpful.

Although it will be some time – if ever – before we reach the record attendance of 3,000 archers at one meeting (as happened in 1583) more and more archers are flocking to tournaments, and it is wise to apply for application forms early. Fees now vary from around 75p to £1 in Britain, and can be substantial in the US; they are not refunded when acts of God drown all hopes of shooting. The number of indoor tournaments is increasing; they are shot in the winter and early spring, are fun and guaranteed dry. The ranges may be short, but the target faces are small, and there is usually no backstop behind the targets, except brick walls. Furthermore, the restricted space makes errors not only more noticeable but also more dangerous. Loosing while the arrow is off the rest could be fatal – as it very nearly was at one tournament; an inch or two more to one side, and it would have been an arrow through the heart instead of through the lung. Indoor shoots are definitely not for nervous beginners.

How far you will have to travel for tournaments will depend on you. Given time and money, you could attend one tournament a week from May to October. Archers travel from Ireland to attend

Indoor shoot

meetings in London; one meets in Kent archers last seen in Dorset; and there is no reason why your club should not challenge Continental clubs for home and away matches. You could average two tournaments a month without having to drive more than an hour or two.

Tournament routine is not very different from a well organised target day, except that everything is on a larger scale. The 'Lady

Paramount' who hands out the prizes (a custom dating from medieval times) may be the mayor's wife or a Lady in her own right. Besides the field captain and target captains there will be a judge, who has the final say in doubtful scores. You are asked to sign in as you arrive, and are expected to attend the final ceremony, even if you haven't won anything. (Had we listened to our inclination at our last tournament, we would have gone home early, but *without* a bottle of sherry, a bottle of wine and a flagon of cider!)

One last word for club secretaries or appropriate committees: PLEASE do not allow any of your members to come dressed in oily jeans and sweaters last used for decorating! This is a new and most regrettable trend, encouraged by an equally new fear of 'interfering with personal liberties!' The colours are GREEN AND/OR WHITE and anyone who can afford modern tackle can buy suitable clothes. (See GNAS *Rules of Shooting*, Appendix E5.)

Governing Bodies of Archery

FITA

The Fédération Internationale de Tir à l'Arc was founded in 1951. Its main objects are to promote and encourage archery throughout the world, to arrange for the organisation of world championships (held biennially), and to confirm and maintain world record scores. Its seat is now in Britain, as its secretary-general is a British subject residing in the United Kingdom. Its administration and control are in the hands of a congress, an administration council and an executive committee. FITA will be in control of the technical side of archery at the next Olympic Games in 1976. There are now about fifty affiliated nations.

GNAS

The first British national championship meeting was held at York in 1844 under the name of The Grand National Archery Meeting. This meeting and the following national meetings were organised by self-appointed committees until 1861, when regional associations were invited to join in the formation of a more democratic body. The name given to the new society has not changed but, in 1950, the Grand National Archery Society adopted a new constitution. Its main objects are to promote archery throughout the United Kingdom, hold a yearly national championship, control the selection and management of British teams competing in international tournaments, and lay down the shooting regulations for the area under its jurisdiction. It is also responsible for national and regional coaching organisations.

The GNAS National Council is made up of: A president, four vice-presidents (two ladies), a chairman, a secretary and/or treasurer, regional representatives, chairmen of committees not already members of the national council, a public relations officer and the retiring chairman (for one year).

There are at the moment eight committees:

1. Finances and General Purposes.
2. Shooting (rules etc).
3. International (FITA).
4. Selection.
5. Juniors.
6. Coaching.
7. Field archery.
8. Olympic Games.

The GNAS publishes a *Bulletin* which is sent to member clubs and associations.

The US official body was founded shortly after the GNAS. The NAA (National Archery Association) was formed in Crawfordsville, Indiana, in 1879, the year of the first national tournament in Chicago.

Owing to their constitutions and to the great amount of work imposed on both honorary officers, GNAS and NAA must be conservative bodies. Newcomers who would like to see swift changes made in tournament regulations, coaching schemes or in other spheres will be disappointed. All proposals must be made from club to county, from county to region and from region to national council. Suggestions do get passed on up the ladder, but impatience will inevitably lead to frustration. Although it may sometimes be a little irritating, this natural defence against hurried innovations may perhaps be a blessing in disguise. Archery, so far, remains one of the very few sports where commonsense, dignity and *enjoyment* prevail, right up to international competition level.

7 A Short History of Archery

The Weapon

Search as you may, you cannot find bows and arrows among the
Polynesian, Micronesian or Australian aborigines. Being such sociable
people, they perhaps preferred clubs. But throughout the rest of the
globe, archery was invented, perhaps several times over in various
places, as long as 30,000 years ago. There are a few very clear
prehistoric drawings in some Spanish caves, showing bows being used
(with excellent examples of the 'drawing unit'). So we can say that as
early as the late Paleolithic period man knew how to kill game from a
safe distance. This achievement is ranked in the *Encyclopaedia Britannica*

as a step equal in importance to the discovery of fire and the wheel.

We in the West have a quaint, rather provincial way of using the word 'prehistoric'. In the days when we were nothing but hairy savages living in smoke-filled caverns, Confucius was already giving dignified lectures on the spiritual value of archery. By 1900 BC, the Chinese Pentagon had already developed this noble sport into an effective means of mass destruction.

In fact, 'European toxophilites' lagged behind for centuries, while the Middle East, the Far East and Africa perfected both skill and equipment to a degree we are only now beginning to reach. Composite and metal bows existed in Biblical times, and our big-game records do not seem all that remarkable when you consider that an Egyptian Pharaoh's expedition killed some 120 elephants! Another Pharaoh, the young Tutankhamun, was buried with his treasured bows, all *twenty-seven* of them! Let this be a lesson to our archery dealers; had they not been so slow off the mark they could have set up a lucrative business on the banks of the Nile.

As for 'technique', it must be remembered that the anchor point used in modern target archery is a fairly recent development. The more natural long draw to the side of the face or even the shoulder was the norm, hence the danger for well built ladies. Drawing to the shoulder must have been the reason why the Thracian female warriors had to amputate one of their breasts.

Nor did ancient archers have adjustable sights, cut-past-centre windows and exterior or interior stabilisers, while the matching of their arrows was probably well below the standard of a set of XX75! Our comparative superiority lies mostly in the *consistency* necessary for shooting the Rounds. Most target archers could not hit a pumpkin off a cow's rump with a longbow. As for shooting astride a galloping mount – the usual practice for Genghis Khan's horsemen – how many GNAS members have tried it? But the Mongols had no monopoly of the combined skills of horsemanship and archery. Babylonian, Persian, Scythian and Assyrian horsemen have been depicted hunting and fighting with short composite bows. More recently, the Red Indians of North America used to bring down buffalo and the odd paleface in the same fashion, and it is interesting to note that they, together with their own adaptation of the bow, originated from Asian lands. If we could then, just for once, draw a curved arrow, we would see that the development of archery as an efficient weapon started round the Persian Gulf and moved chiefly towards the Far East and north, drifting eventually across the Bering Straights to conquer the wilderness of America. We could also draw two small arrows, with their nocking points still on the Persian Gulf, but pointing north-west to Greece and south-west to Egypt.

The Roman army had its Cretan archers, and there were promising archers in Arabia and Turkey, but we must now move to the British Isles.

'La fleur des archiers du monde'

Some will say that the Danes introduced the bow into England. They may have; but they, together with the Saxons, thought it a rather vulgar method of fighting and only fit for amusement. In fact, the Danes used King Edmund of East Anglia for target practice, satisfied that it was the lowest possible form of insult they could inflict upon him. This ungentlemanly execution was performed in AD 870, but reference was made to Welsh archers in 633. It would seem that the famous hill-dwellers of old not only showed superiority in music and poetry but were the first to use the bow with devastating effect in Britain. Their arrows could pierce oak doors 4in thick and nail mounted men to their horses. It was the Saxons who discovered, with unexpected chagrin, that 'arrows, moving as quietly as breath', were raining heavily in the Welsh valleys. On their first encounter with the natives, they had to flee without even making contact.

An intelligent interest in archery followed the initial shock and, eventually, Saxons and Welsh Nationalists agreed to combine against the Normans. By encouraging the spread of archery throughout the land, this early collaboration was to lead to the conquest of Ireland in the twelfth century and, later, to the victories of Crécy, Poitiers and Agincourt.

During the glorious days of English archery, however, it was the commoner's field of action not the noble's. War was not a gentleman's pastime unless it could be waged astride a charger and the enemy beaten down with hefty swords. However, the commoners, more down to earth, were free of such romantic notions. It was obviously better to stop the opponent dead in his tracks at 12 score yards than to run the risk of falling off a horse in the midst of battle –

a mere heap of helpless ironmongery ('. . . and he that was once down could not be raised again without great succour and aid'). Moreover, a bow was cheaper than a suit of armour and a charger.

It was indeed the commoner, lifted to the status of Yeoman of England, who made up for the discrepancy between the numbers of the English and French knights at Crécy, Poitiers and Agincourt. At Crécy in 1346, in spite of the 15,000 Genoese mercenaries hired by the French and marching forwards with ugly shouts and lethal crossbows, the 600 English archers 'stirred not for all that'; and, after taking a volley of bolts from the enemy they 'stepped forth one pace and let fly their arrows so wholly and so thick that it seemed snow'. Again and again the French knights were frustrated in their eagerness to come to grips. 'The French King would have fain have come thither . . . , but there was a great hedge of archers before him.'

Trained from early childhood, English archers could draw a 100lb bow with ease and kill a single enemy at 80 or 100yd. In the midst of battle they could shoot twelve arrows a minute, and were disappointed if they missed once. But their real devastating power rested in volley firing, or 'softening up' the enemy. This tactic was first tried by William the Conqueror at Hastings and perfected during the English victories in the Hundred Years War.

But in ancient even more than in modern warfare, skill in handling efficient weapons would have counted for little without the courage of the men using them. The chronicles of Jean Froissart describe the feats of the English archers with a notable absence of chauvinism. At Poitiers in 1356 they again showed their valour, doing 'their company a great advantage, for they shot so thick that the Frenchmen wist not on what side to take heed'. They repelled the French knights seventeen times without even breaking ranks, and repeated their heroic feats at Agincourt in 1415, where they had to fight the enemy within as well as without, so to speak, being distracted by hunger and dysentery.

Decline of Archery in Warfare

However, English warlords cannot have been fired by the hymn that was sung in India some 1,000 years before Christ: 'With the bow let us conquer every quarter of the World.' After Agincourt, no great Continental battles were fought with archery playing a major role. In fact, as a military weapon, it declined steadily until its final fling at the siege of Worcester in 1651. Although the musket and arquebus replaced the bow as light-infantry weapons they remained inferior to it for a very long time. Bows had an effective range of 240yd and archers could line up ten deep; firing muskets was a slow job which could only be done in two or three ranks. The main reason for the adoption of the new weapons was time-saving: it only took a few days to train a soldier in the use of firearms, while an archer had to practise from childhood.

Various rulers, notably Henry VIII, tried to arrest the decline of archery by displaying their own interest in toxophily and by imposing laws and decrees when that method failed – but to no avail. By the middle of the seventeenth century, the bow and arrow, as a significant military weapon, had had its day.

But, on a more limited scale, the silent killer is still used. A nun was mortally hit during the Congo troubles and, even more recently, a policeman was shot in India. In World War II, British commandos using short steel bows despatched a few German sentries and, should the Nazis have invaded England, they would have suffered casualties in the hands of Peter Fleming's resistance fighters, trained in the use of the longbow. And why not? Many a time have I wished for good archery tackle when serving with the French Maquis. Polish archers on horseback stung Napoleon's troops in 1807, and North Vietnamese are known to have killed helicopter pilots with crossbows. With the march of time, archers have changed camps: once the mighty, they are now the guerillas, but their weapon is still to be reckoned with.

The Sport

Preparation for battle used to be a good way to keep fit and alert; with today's forms of warfare, it isn't. However, it is still possible to derive beneficial enjoyment from a few 'war sports' without killing anyone. The best of these sports are two which were practised centuries ago: fencing and archery.

'The Fayre Shootynge'

Even when the bow and arrow had its grim usefulness, archery was enjoyed for peaceful relaxation. In the Middle Ages, festivities included archery competitions where the targets sometimes consisted of garlands of roses hanging from trees. The winners were presented with prizes which could range from gloves to white bulls or even saddled and bridled mounts. Champions then were as much idolised by the public as are today's football stars. On popular archery fields, one learns, grass was known to stop growing through the 'constant raking by missed arrows'. I wonder whether this should perhaps be rewritten as 'the constant raking *for lost* arrows!'

The butts were usually made of turf, with the centre of target white. A good shot was not 'in the Gold', but 'in the blanc'.

The appeal of archery then was by no means limited to the humble. Queens and kings enjoyed it, Bishops advised it, headmasters enforced it and it even inspired Roger Ascham to write the very first treatise about a sport ever written in English. His book, *Toxophilus*, first published in 1545, was reprinted as recently as 1968. In fact in the sixteenth century, archery, as a sport, reached a peak which would not be equalled until the latter half of our century. But while the weapon suffered fatal insults from new war toys, the sport was rudely dislodged by a new passion, which swept through the fickle populace like wild fire: shove ha'penny! Hierarchies tried to forbid the 'sinful game' as they had tried to forbid the use of a crossbow and arbalests, but to no avail.

Not long after Henry bought a shooting glove for Anne Boleyn, archery began to lose its popularity. From Henry's day to the end of World War II, archery simmered gently in a few lovingly tendered cauldrons.

'The Noble and useful Recreation of Archery, for many years neglected'

The first of the early societies to which we owe its survival was The Kilwinning Archers, founded in Scotland in 1483. Later came The Fraternity of St Georges, in 1537, and the Finsbury Archers in 1658.

In 1676, the long climb back to recognition began with the formation of The Queen's Bodyguard for Scotland, or Royal Company of Archers. They, together with The Royal Toxophilite Society (1781) and The Woodmen of Arden (1785) are still in existence today. Indeed, the Royal Tox and the Woodmen have shot against each other since 1878, and the Royal Company of Archers can show their match results for every year since 1875.

In the US, a wide and enthusiastic interest in archery was first encouraged by the American writer Maurice Thompson in 1878 while another author, Dr Saxton Pope, did likewise for hunting and field archery in the beginning of the twentieth century.

During this first revival, the enjoyment of archery was known only to a privileged few — a situation perhaps comparable to that of polo today. Robert Burns and Raeburn shot, but Mr Jones the baker no longer did, or did not yet. Even in 1945, there were no more than a dozen clubs in England. Then came the great American post-war bubbling. Although it was stated in 1954 that 'the number of American Archers having reached the peak of one and a half [American] million, the post-war boom may be nearly over', in 1958 the number had risen to 7,500,000 (8 to 10 million according to the *New Yorker*). In 1969, 60,000 permits were issued for hunting with bows and arrows in the state of Michigan alone!

Perhaps we could end this display of statistics with a last example of the danger of making bold statements: 'The use of the musket has become so general that Archery . . . has little chance of recovering its popularity.' The author of these gloomy lines could not have known that just over a century later, thirty countries would meet in Holland for the 24th World Archery Championships. The contest took three days and sixty-six targets were used. At the 25th World Championships in Pennsylvania, contestants came from nations as far apart as Mongolia and Mexico, Norway and Spain and Russia and South Africa.

Whither Now?

Judging from the trend in the late 60s and early 70s, archery is undergoing one of its periodical comebacks, perhaps an unprecedented one. How will it be affected by its growing popularity in our modern times? There are some obvious dangers. Greater reliance on technological aids and the stresses of international competition may perhaps improve both performance and equipment, but can also destroy pleasure. Taking another sport as an example, it is a melancholy thought to recall the tremendous exhilaration and fun of the early ski races through virgin snow. Now you wear a helmet and speed down prepared runs. Should you straighten up from the egg position or take off on a bump, you will increase your time by a fraction of a second — and lose the race. Nor does being packed like sardines in a cable car or freezing to death in a chair-lift compare favourably with the leisurely climb in the fairy-like glory of untrodden slopes.

Still taking a pessimistic view, we might commercialise archery and end up with shooting alleys where thousands of 'archers' will send arrows flying to the blaring of canned music. We might also perfect the prostitution of a once dignified sport by introducing big cash prizes in indoor tournaments, sponsored by the NEWEST biological detergent. Modern science is a wondrous thing; it would be no trouble at all to fix an electronic homing device within the pile of the arrow. A machine would draw your 200lb bow and you could trigger your automatic loose while watching TV and drinking Coke. What a thrill it would be to know that you could hit the Gold repeatedly at 1,000 yards! Or would it?

Looking on the brighter side we have the fact that archery is not, and never will be, a spectator sport. It thus stands a good chance of remaining untouched by mass hysteria or commercialism. The most hopeful factor in the future of archery is the intimate, quietly passionate relationship of man and bow. The cynic will say that archery is not a sport; it is an incurable disease. But, deep down, we all know what archery really is – a friend, a spouse or a lover, perhaps the three rolled into one; a companion whose rewards are not granted to the fickle. It has the power to toss a man from happiness into despair and back again without ever losing his love or respect.

So, Yorks and FITAs may come and go and technology may impose passing fashions; but as long as two or three men can find a green lawn on which to bend their bows, true archery should survive. After all, it has done so for some thirty thousand years.

Glossary

Anchor Point: a particular location on the archer's face where his drawing hand will be 'anchored' before he releases the arrow.

Arrow Rest: plastic or feather attachment fixed above the arrow shelf.

Arrow Shelf: part of the bow protruding or cut away above the handle, usually unsuitable to rest the arrow on and not found on self bows.

Back: side of the bow facing away from the archer.

Belly: side of the bow facing the archer.

Blunt: A blunt arrowhead for hunting small game or dislodging the wooden birds of a Popinjay mast.

Bolt: the short 'arrow' used with crossbows.

Boss: the conventional, circular target without the target face; made of a coil of straw.

Bouncer: an arrow which does not penetrate the target sufficiently to stay on it.

Bowsight: device fixed on the back or belly of the bow, enabling the archer to aim directly at the target, whatever the distance.

Brace (to): to string the bow.

Bracer: arm-guard.

Bracing Height: distance from the bow to the string when the bow is braced; usually taken from back of bow to nocking point.

Broadhead: razor-sharp arrowhead used for hunting big game.

Brushnock: rubber 'cushion' placed near the tips of the bow just below the string loops to prevent branches being caught in the string while hunting, or simply to quieten a 'noisy' bow.

Butt: the original mound of turf at which archers used to shoot, or any backing for targets other than the conventional round boss.

Butts: field where archers meet regularly for shooting.

Cast: word used fairly loosely, which could mean the speed imparted to the arrow, the distance at which the bow will shoot or the degree of flatness of the trajectory (the stronger and shorter the bow is, the 'flatter the cast').

Chrysal: crack in the belly of the bow.

Clout: old English word for 'cloth'; small white flag or circular target for long-distance shooting.

Clout Shoot: competition where men shoot at the clout from 9-score yards and women from 6-score yards.

Cock Feather: feather placed at right-angles to the arrow nock, usually of a different colour from the other two.

Composite bow: bow made of more than one material (wood, horn and sinews in ancient bows, wood and fibreglass in modern bows).

Creeping: allowing the arrow to move forward after the draw and before the loose.

Cresting: identification marks on the arrow, usually near the fletching.

End: number of arrows shot before the score is taken, usually six or three.

Face: painted scoring surface fixed on the boss, made of canvas, jute, sailcloth or paper.

Fast: call to archers meaning: 'Danger, stop shooting!' From: 'Stand fast!'

Fistmele: old measurement for bracing height of wooden bows (closed fist and outstretched thumb).

Fletching: plastic or feather vanes placed near the nock to steady the arrow flight.

Flu-flu: arrow with one 8in feather fixed spirally round the shaft; for very short ranges, shooting at birds or squirrels.

Ground Quiver: metal support stuck in the ground. It can hold arrows but is mostly used to rest the bow on between ends.

Hanger: arrow which has not penetrated the boss but is still held by the target face, hanging across the target.

Holding: pause between drawing and loosing.

Instinctive Shooting: shooting without the help of a sighting device.

Kisser: small protuberance on the string, felt by the lips at full draw; made with tape, rubber or plastic, it helps consistency in draw and elevation.

Let Down (to): the act of slowly releasing tension at full draw without loosing the arrow.

Limb: upper or lower half of the bow.

Loose: loosing, or the way or style in which this is done.

Loosing: act of releasing string and arrow when the string is drawn.

Mark: object or victim at which the archer is aiming.

Nock: groove in the bow or slot in the arrow in which the string is engaged.

Nock (to): to secure the arrow on the string, prior to drawing.

Nocking Point: the exact spot on the string where the arrow should be nocked.

Nocklocks: rubber beads sometimes used on bowstrings to locate the nocking point.

Overbowed: of an archer with too strong a bow.

Pair: three arrows.

Perfect End: six arrows in the Gold.

Petticoat: part of the target face outside the scoring area.

Pile: tip of the arrow, conical or oval in shape, usually socketed into the shaft.

Pin Hole: exact centre of the target.

Point Blank Shooting: distance at which you can aim with the pile of the arrow on the Gold.

Point of Aim: aiming mark below or above the target.

Poker: stabilizing rod screwed into the bow.

Quiver: from the French *cuivre*, a case designed to hold six arrows; suspended from the belt or strapped round the shoulder.

Riser: the wide part in the middle of the bow; the extra piece of wood on the belly of wooden bows.

Self Bow: bow made of one piece of wood.

Serving: about 6 to 8in of extra thread round the middle of the string.

Shaft: the arrow itself, or length of arrow between pile and nock.

Shooting in a Bow: correct expression for 'to shoot with a bow'.

Sight Mark: a line on the bow or on the sight track used to aim at a certain distance.

Snake: of an arrow which has buried itself under grass.

Spine: degree of stiffness of an arrow.

Sweet: of a bow which draws smoothly and shoots quietly.

Tab: piece of leather that protects the drawing fingers and ensures a smooth release.

Tackle: archery equipment.

Tassel: to clean muddy arrows; usually green wool, and can be made with club colours and registered with the GNAS.

Toxophilite: one who practises archery and is interested in all its aspects, including its history.

Underbowed: of an archer with too weak a bow.

Vane: Section of feather or plastic that makes up the fletching.

Weight. *(a)* **draw-weight:** measurement of the pull needed to draw the full length of an arrow, eg 36lb at 28in. *(b)* **weight in hand:** physical weight of the bow.

Window. *(a)* **archer's:** space sometimes seen between the string and the side of the bow. *(b)* **bow's:** the cut-away portion above the handle of a composite or fibreglass bow.

Appendix

(a) Publications Necessary to Club Secretaries, and Recommended to all Members

The Grand National Archery Society, *Rules of Shooting*.

The National Archery Association of the United States, *Official Tournament Rules*.

International Archery Federation (FITA), *Official Shooting Rules*.

Field Archery Handbook.

Handicap Tables.

Bowman's Handbook, edited by Patrick Clover.

(All available from archery shops)

The British Archer (magazine), editor Patrick Clover, 68 The Dale, Widley, Portsmouth PO7 5DE, England.

Archery World (official publication of the NAA), 534 N Broadway, Milwaukee, Wisconsin 53202, USA.

Bow & Arrow, 116 E Badillo, Covina, California 91722, USA.

(b) Archery Courses

Write to GNAS or NAA Secretary, or to: Central Council of Physical Recreation, 160 Great Portland Street, London W1N 5TB.

Further Reading

Ascham, Roger, *Toxophilus* (1545, reprinted 1968).

Bilson, F. *Bowmanship* (1965).

— *Crossbows* (1974).

Butler, F. D. *The New Archery* (1968).

Clover, P. *Bowman's Handbook* (1957, revised 1968).

Forbes, T. A. *New Guide to Better Archery* (New York and London, 1962).

Gillelan, G. H. *Modern ABCs of Bow and Arrow* (Harrisburg, Pa, 1968).

— *Archery for Boys and Girls* (Chicago, 1965).

Gordon and Grimley, *The Book of the Bow* (1958).

Heath, E. G. *Archery, the Modern Approach* (New York and London, 1966).

Keaggy, D. J. *Power Archery* (reprinted 1968).

Laycock, G. and Bauer, E. *Hunting with Bow and Arrow* (New York and London, 1965).

McKinney, W. C. *Archery* (Dubuque, Iowa, 1966).

Milliken, E. K. *Archery in the Middle Ages* (1967).

Richardson, M. E. *Teach Yourself Archery* (1961).

Sigler, H. T. *Pocket Guide to Archery* (Harrisburg, Pa, 1967).

Thompson, M. and W. H. *How to Train in Archery* (1879).

Wiseman, H. *Tackle Archery this Way* (1959).

Acknowledgements

'Research' is a pleasing word which authors like to use to describe one of their activities. In fact, it means borrowing information probably already borrowed from former scholars who had to work really hard, borrowing from a great many writers who. . . . To this throng of authors looking over my shoulder I offer my sincere thanks for the enjoyable hours spent in libraries. They are also fully responsible for the historical references appearing in this book, as well as for the data in the last chapter.

In more tangible fashion, I would also like to express my gratitude to the Grand National Archery Society for the extracts from their Book of Rules and Handicap Tables, to my American friends for putting me right on a few points, to the editor of *The British Archer* for finding suitable photographs and photographers, and to a little photographer's shop in St Leonards on Sea who processed my films so expertly. I am also much indebted to Mr D. G. Quick for the sound counsel he so willingly gave me.

But I doubt that this book would have ever been written, were it not for my friends of *The Friars Gate Archers*. With them I shared in the exciting adventure of forming a new archery club, and, with them, I have learnt more than I would have learnt from a thousand books.

D.R.

Index

Aiming, 52, 54–5, 58–60, 68
Anchor point, 41
Archer's paradox, 35–6
Archery darts, 14, 16
  golf, 11–12, 15
Arrows, 19, 22, 30, 35
  withdrawing, 77–8

Bare-bows, 18, 69
Bows, 19–21, 29, 31–5, 37
Bowsling, 39
Bowstring, 28, 38
Bracer, 22–3
Bracing the bow, 20–1, 50–2
Bracing height, 65
  gauge, 47
Brushnocks, 45

Cast, 32, 45
Classification scheme, 102–4
Clout shooting, 12
Clicker, 36, 40
Club, 47, 70–94
Clothing, 45
Coaching, 85–6

Displays, 89, 92
Drawing, 32–4, 36, 54–7
Draw-length, 21–2, 31–2
Draw-weight, 21, 32

Equipment, 18–45, 76–7, 84
Etiquette, 74–5
Eye, dominant, 50

Fédération Internationale de Tir à l'Arc,
  71, 108
Field, 80–3
  for display, 91
Field archery, 9–10, 47, 67, 69
Field captain, 88, 100
Finances, 83
Fishing, 14

Fletching, 37
  'flu', 13
Fletching jig, 37
Flight shooting, 11
Follow-through, 41, 44, 58

Glove, 25
Grand National Archery
  Society, 71, 108–9
Gold shyness, 40, 59
Grand Master Bowman, 102
Grip, 52–3, 59

Handicap system, 102–4
Hunting, 13–14

Instinctive shooting, 67–9
Insurance, 83

Juniors, 84, 93–4, 106
Junior rounds, 105

Keeper, glove, 25
Klicker, see Clicker
Kisser, 59

Loose, 41, 58

Master Bowman, 102
Matches, 87–9

National American Association, 109
Nocking, 26–7, 53
Nocklocks, 45
Nocking point, 28, 38
Novelty shoots, 14, 90

Petticoat, 9
Pinhole, 9
Popinjay, 12–13
Power archery, 66–7

Quivers, 25, 28, 30

Rounds, 9–10, 85, 96–103
Roving, 16

Safety rules, 22, 49–50, 89
Schools, archery in, 93–4
Scoring, 100–2
Score book, 31, 102–3
Season, shooting, 47
Serving, 38
Shooting line, 52
Sights, 38–9
Spine, arrow, 35, 37
Stabilisers, 36, 40, 44
Stance, 67
Straightening aids, arrow, 37
String keeper, 43–4

Suscriptions, 93

Tab, 23, 25
Target archery, 9–11, 14–15
Target day, 85
Target captain, 85, 100
Target stand, 19
Targets, 9, 11, 19
   carrying, 77, 79
Technique, 46–69
   correction of, 63–4
Tournaments, 9, 97, 101, 104–8

Weather, effects of, 62–3
Window, archer's, 59

Zones (target face), 11

David & Charles have a book on it

Crossbows by Frank Bilson. For many people the urge to shoot is stifled by the rising cost of going out with the guns. Competitive target shooting with one of man's earliest weapons – the crossbow – is proving an excellent alternative. In the first book to be written on crossbows since the beginning of the century. Frank Bilson provides a fascinatingly detailed introduction to a sport which is fast gaining new enthusiasts throughout the world. Illustrated.

UNIFORM WITH THIS VOLUME: The Art of Good Shooting by J. E. M. Ruffer (Royal Marine Retd). The complete guide to marksmanship and proficiency with the shotgun, written by a practised shot and experienced coach. The accent is on common sense and etiquette, with an underlying no-nonsense approach to the art of hitting the target cleanly and easily. Even the most experienced shots will benefit from this book and its constant reminders of easily-forgotten essentials. Illustrated.

A Guide to Rough Shooting, by Arthur Cadman. An authority on British deer and wildfowl distils years of experience of shooting over every kind of rough ground. A book of particular value to the young shot, to whom is devoted a special chapter. Well laced with amusing and often informative anecdotes. Illustrated.

Training Pointers and Setters by J. B. Maurice. That the ancient art of training gundogs can be learned from a book is ably demonstrated by Dr Maurice, who has himself had considerable successes with pointers and setters. He covers breeding, choosing a puppy, domestication and health hazards, and the basics of educating a gundog for a typical shooting day. Illustrated.

Still-Water Angling by Richard Walker. Hailed as revolutionary when it first appeared in 1953, this book is still a firmly-established classic of angling literature. This new edition incorporates much additional information gleaned by the author and his friends since the book was first published. Illustrated.

By River, Stream and Loch: Thirty Years with a Trout Rod by A. R. B. Haldane. With its delightful wood-cuts by Helen Monro Turner, this is a book written entirely for pleasure, and the quality of the writing makes angling exciting and intelligible to non-anglers as well. Illustrated.

Coarse Fishing for New Anglers by W. M. Hill. A practical introduction to the sport of coarse fishing for keen beginners of all ages, this book has been designed to take the reader easily and interestingly through the progressive stages of his angling apprenticeship – an ideal guide to one of the most popular of all outdoor sports, and an introduction to the hobby of a lifetime. Illustrated.

THE FIELD Bedside Book 4, edited by Wilson Stephens. Another selection of the most popular articles from two years' issues of *The Field* magazine, with styles ranging from the straightforward and gently reflective to tongue in cheek and downright amusing. The perfect gift and an ideal read for all lovers of the countryside and its ways.